The Giant Book of Odd Facts

By
Jake Jacobs

Kindle Edition

* * * * *

Published by Jake Jacobs at Amazon Kindle

1.

Some numbers are illegal.

Reference: (https://en.wikipedia.org/wiki/Illegal_prime)

2.

Food Network's "Chopped" was originally supposed to be set in a mansion with the host being a butler. The butler was also to be holding a Chihuahua and when a chef was chopped, the losing dish was fed to the Chihuahua.

Reference: (https://www.mediaite.com/food/ted-allen-chopped-butler-chihuahua/)

3.

Brazil has 49 prisons with no guards, where a system of self-rule among inmates has proved a success. These prisons are cheaper to run, have lower rates of recidivism, and are designed to benefit the wider community.

Reference: (https://www.theguardian.com/global-development/2018/apr/02/no-thought-of-escaping-inside-brazilian-prisons-with-no-guards)

4.

A Turing Machine can be explained as a choose your own adventure book.

Reference: (https://www.youtube.com/watch?v=-ZS_zFg4w5k)

5.

The father of modern art in Thailand is an Italian sculptor named Corrado Feroci who constructed many famous Thai monuments, opened a renowned art school in Bangkok, and became a Thai citizen after Italy surrendered to the allies to avoid capture by the occupying Japanese.

Reference: (https://en.wikipedia.org/wiki/Silpa_Bhirasri)

6.

The sunscreen rating SPF 15 means $1/15^{th}$ of the UV-B radiation is not blocked. SPF 30 means $1/30^{th}$.

Reference: (https://en.wikipedia.org/wiki/Sunscreen#Sun_Protection_Factor)

7.

Pessimism is one of the key symptoms of depression, and depressed people are more pessimistic when predicting the future than non-depressed people, even when they are given the exact same information with which to make their predictions.

Reference: (https://effectiviology.com/pessimism-bias/)

8.

The pilot episode for the game show "You're in the Picture" went so poorly that Jackie Gleason used the time slot to apologize for a half hour the following week.

Reference: (http://www.vulture.com/2012/01/jackie-gleasons-half-hour-apology-and-youre-in-the-picture-the-show-that-warranted-it.html)

9.

Snapchat trolled Facebook on April Fool's Day with a "Facebook" filter, designed to recreate Russian bots on Facebook deployed during the 2016 U.S. Presidential election. The filter placed a Facebook UI around the photo with Cyrillic script-like text and showed likes from "your mum" and "a bot".

Reference: (https://www.theverge.com/2018/4/1/17185566/snapchat-april-fools-facebook-russian-bot-filter)

10.

WWE's The Undertaker is afraid of cucumbers. Paul Bearer watched The Undertaker, "throw up all over a Waffle House because there was a cucumber floating in his iced tea." Bearer used to prank the Deadman by placing cucumber slices in his hat and gloves.

Reference: (https://nypost.com/2017/07/31/undertaker-is-deathly-afraid-of-cucumbers-and-wwe-foes-tortured-him/)

11.

People from the lower classes in the mountain region of Austria consumed arsenic as a health tonic or for cosmetic purposes and became dependent to an amount that could kill a normal person.

Reference: (http://ultimatehistoryproject.com/arsenic-eaters.html)

12.

An MS-13 gang boss tried to get the gang into drug smuggling in the early 2000s, but had to split off because the gang members resisted putting personal profit ahead of the collective, and were inept.

Reference: (http://www.newsweek.com/ms-13-donald-trump-jeff-sessions-gang-gangs-immigration-drug-cartel-mexico-855926)

13.

Thailand uses the Buddhist calendar rather than the Gregorian calendar typically used by western-influenced countries, which is 543 years ahead of the latter. That means the current year in Thailand is 2561 BE rather than 2018 CE.

Reference: (https://en.wikipedia.org/wiki/Date_and_time_notation_in_Thailand)

14.

In 1974, the city of Tanner, Alabama, was hit by 2 F5 tornadoes in 30 minutes. A man injured in the first tornado was taken to a church in the area, which collapsed in the second tornado, killing him.

Reference:(https://en.wikipedia.org/wiki/1974_Super_Outbreak#Tanner,_Alabama_(1st_tornado))

15.

Although there are more stars in the universe than the grains of sand on Earth, there are more atoms in your body than all the stars in the observable universe.

Reference: (http://wafflesatnoon.com/stars-vs-sand-vs-human-atoms-vs-insects/)

16.

The Philippines has bread called "tasty bread", which is simply a sliced loaf or sandwich bread.

Reference: (https://www.thespruceeats.com/inside-a-filipino-panaderia-3030321)

17.

The phrase "Eddie would go" is about the Hawaiian legend and lifeguard Eddie Aikau who was famous for surfing and saving people from big waves on the North Shore. When no one would go, Eddie would go.

Reference: (https://en.wikipedia.org/wiki/Eddie_Aikau#Popular_culture)

18.

In 2009, Latvian fire crews were called to a meteorite fall, which left a 20 meter burning crater. This created huge interest, but turned out to be a PR stunt for a new phone tariff. The PR company was shamed by the media, fines were levied, but the PR company won several awards as a result.

Reference: (https://en.wikipedia.org/wiki/2009_Latvian_meteorite_hoax)

19.

There are no mosquitos in Iceland.

Reference: (http://icelandmag.is/article/reason-non-existence-mosquitoes-iceland)

20.

McGuire's Irish Pub is a popular landmark in Florida where the walls and the ceiling are covered with thousands of autographed dollar bills whose collective value has been estimated to over one million dollars.

Reference: (http://www.amusingplanet.com/2015/02/the-million-dollar-mcguire-irish-pub.html)

21.

The Tasmanian devil has the most powerful bite relative to body size of any living mammalian carnivore, exerting a force of 553 Newtons.

Reference: (https://en.wikipedia.org/wiki/Tasmanian_devil)

22.

The International Fixed Calendar has 13 months with 28 days each. This makes every month perfectly divisible into 4 weeks and always starting on a Sunday and ending on a Saturday.

Reference: (http://internationalfixedcalendar.com/)

23.

The stump-jump plough was a plough invented in South Australia in the late 19th century to solve the particular problem of preparing mallee lands for cultivation.

Reference: (https://en.wikipedia.org/wiki/Stump-jump_plough)

24.

Madame Tussaud, of Wax Museum fame, was an artist in the court of Louis XVI and Marie Antoinette. During the French Revolution, she was forced to make wax death masks of both of their faces immediately after they were guillotined.

Reference: (http://blog.raucousroyals.com/2009/01/madame-tussaud-witness-to-revolution.html?m=1)

25.

Shrikes is a type of bird that is known for impaling their still-living prey on a plant's thorns to save for later, store for their offspring, or attract mates.

Reference: (https://video.nationalgeographic.com/video/weirdest-shrike)

26.

Recently, many people reported experiencing a reaction to eating pine nuts called "pine nut syndrome". It results in a bad, metallic taste in their mouth that is heightened by sugar for 2 to 14 days. It can appear even if you have eaten them you're whole life.

Reference: (https://www.latimes.com/local/abcarian/la-me-ra-bad-taste-in-my-mouth--20140722-column.html%3foutputType=amp)

27.

Male calico cats are rare because of a genetic defect called Trisomy.

Reference: (https://www.mnn.com/family/pets/stories/why-are-male-calico-cats-so-rare)

28.

Before 1877, music listeners could only listen to their favorite songs when someone else was playing them, whether in a concert hall or at home.

Reference: (https://www.makeuseof.com/tag/the-evolution-of-music-consumption-how-we-got-here/)

29.

China's one child policy, introduced in 1979, prevented the birth of 400 million people, as well as generated up to two trillion in fines.

Reference: (http://www.bbc.com/news/magazine-34666440)

30.

Western Arnhem Land, Australia, is home to some of the most significant rock art in the world. It has arguably the world's longest continuing artistic traditions, with rock art dating back thousands of years and still being produced today.

Reference: (https://en.wikipedia.org/wiki/Gunbalanya,_Northern_Territory)

31.

Flight attendants do not get paid until the plane leaves the gate.

Reference: (https://money.howstuffworks.com/flight-attendant3.htm)

32.

The Martu Wangka language developed rapidly, permitting a researcher to write a dictionary of the language within two decades, consisting of over 400 pages.

Reference: (https://en.wikipedia.org/wiki/Martu_Wangka)

33.

In 1973, Jerry Lee Lewis played one show at the Grand Ole Opry, which barred both rock & roll and profanity. Jerry kicked off a 40-minute rock & roll show, calling himself a, "rhythm and blues-singin' motherfucker'. It was all revenge on the Nashville scene for his cold welcome in 1955.

Reference: (https://en.wikipedia.org/wiki/Grand_Ole_Opry#1960s)

34.

Gemini 3 was named Molly Brown in the hope that it wouldn't sink at splashdown. NASA didn't like this and asked astronaut Gus Grissom to change the name, to which he replied "how about the Titanic?". NASA relented, but this was the last time astronauts were allowed to name their capsule.

Reference: (https://en.wikipedia.org/wiki/Gemini_3#Flight)

35.

Sea otters hold hands when they sleep so they don't drift apart.

Reference: (https://www.mnn.com/earth-matters/animals/photos/15-fascinating-facts-about-otters/yes-its-true-sea-otters-hold-hands)

36.

The record for shortest number 1 single has stood for close to sixty years.

Reference: (https://www.theindustryobserver.com.au/the-record-for-shortest-1-has-stood-for-close-to-sixty-years/)

37.

Johann Strauss II popularized the term "YOLO" in 1855.

Reference: (https://www.theindustryobserver.com.au/the-origin-story-of-yolo/)

38.

Tim Allen was arrested in 1978 for cocaine possession and served 2 years in prison.

Reference: (https://en.wikipedia.org/wiki/Tim_Allen#Legal_issues)

39.

The Great Pacific Garbage Patch is now 2,000 times the size of New York City, and growing rapidly.

Reference: (https://thebrag.com/trash-island-is/)

40.

One third of all internet traffic from the U.S. to Asia passes through a single skyscraper in Downtown Los Angeles, where 260 ISPs lease space for interconnected networks.

Reference: (https://en.wikipedia.org/wiki/One_Wilshire#cite_note-bcloudbuildings-2)

41.

During the Bahia Incident, a Confederate ship was captured by a Union one in Brazil, meaning that the Civil War was technically also fought in the Southern Hemisphere.

Reference: (https://en.wikipedia.org/wiki/Bahia_incident)

42.

Dr. Samuel Pozzi was a gynecologist and a handsome surgeon. He was well received in Parisian solons in the late 1800s. He had many affairs and, as a consequence, was nicknamed Dr. Love. He was murdered by a patient whose leg he had amputated years prior.

Reference: (https://wikipedia.org/wiki/Samuel_Jean_de_Pozzi)

43.

Former slave Benjamin Banneker, a noted astronomer, wrote a letter accusing Thomas Jefferson of fraud and hypocrisy for championing liberty while owning slaves.

Reference: (https://www.currentaffairs.org/2017/07/why-is-charles-murray-odious)

44.

In 1991, Charlie Sheen became convinced that "Flower of Flesh & Blood," a 1985 Japanese horror movie, was a snuff film and reported it to the FBI. The Bureau dropped the investigation after the movie's producer demonstrated the special effects.

Reference: (https://en.wikipedia.org/wiki/Guinea_Pig_%28film_series%29)

45.

The Newman's Own food company donates 100% of its profits to charity.

Reference: (https://en.wikipedia.org/wiki/Newman%27s_Own)

46.

After Charlotte Corday was executed by guillotine, a man named Legros lifted her head and slapped it on the cheeks, an expression of "unequivocal indignation" then appeared on her face suggesting that victims of the guillotine may retain consciousness for a short while.

Reference: (https://en.wikipedia.org/wiki/Charlotte_Corday)

47.

The actors who portrayed Albus Dumbledore, Sirius Black and Peter Pettigrew, all played Winston Churchill in movies.

Reference: (https://en.wikipedia.org/wiki/Cultural_depictions_of_Winston_Churchill)

48.

Instead of a jail sentence, a Texas man agreed to be sentenced to sleep in an outdoors doghouse for 30 consecutive nights, as a punishment for abusing his son.

Reference: (https://www.chron.com/news/bizarre/article/Vidor-man-sentenced-to-30-days-in-doghouse-2106599.php)

49.

In 1972, President Nixon wanted then Democrat Governor John Connally to succeed him, and even considered forming a new party or renaming the GOP to achieve it.

Reference: (http://articles.baltimoresun.com/1994-05-20/news/1994140195_1_connally-nixon-new-party)

50.

In 2016, the U.S. Government Publishing Office officially recommends the demonym for Indiana be "Hoosier" instead of "Indianan."

Reference: (https://en.wikipedia.org/wiki/List_of_demonyms_for_U.S._states_and_territories)

51.

Half a liter of water contains just over 25 moles of water molecules. A mole of marbles would cover the Earth 3.5 meters deep.

Reference: (https://youtu.be/UI4SSAgYy_s)

52.

The pace car was stolen at Talladega in 1986.

Reference: (https://www.youtube.com/watch?v=ICi3kIzSIZg&feature=youtu.be)

53.

In Alaska there is an ice road from Prudhoe Bay, Alaska, to Point Thomson, Alaska. The ice road is 68 miles, or 109 kilometers, long and is mainly used by semi-trucks to deliver cargo.

Reference: (https://en.wikipedia.org/wiki/Ice_road)

54.

Rye was domesticated by Vavilovian mimicry. The weed-ancestor of rye evolved to closely resemble wheat so that ancient farmers would not remove it from their fields.

Reference: (http://www.indefenseofplants.com/blog/2016/2/2/the-accidental-grain-how-rye-evolved-its-way-into-our-diet)

55.

The Icelandic Naming Committee is a committee that can deny the introduction of any new given child names into the Icelandic culture and vocabulary based on compatibility with Icelandic tradition.

Reference: (https://en.wikipedia.org/wiki/Icelandic_Naming_Committee)

56.

Anti-aliasing refers to the techniques used to deal with signals that become indistinguishable from one another, usually in an image or sound frequency; in computer graphics, this involves making jagged curves or lines smoother in appearance.

Reference: (https://en.wikipedia.org/wiki/Anti-aliasing)

57.

Chicken doesn't need to be cooked to 165 degrees to be safe, rather it just needs to be cooked long enough at certain temperatures to kill off bacteria, which can be achieved at as little as 130 degrees. 165 degrees just kills the bacteria instantly, so the USDA recommends it for simplification.

Reference: (https://www.seriouseats.com/2015/07/the-food-lab-complete-guide-to-sous-vide-chicken-breast.html)

58.

Vacuum Decay, the Universe's theoretical "self-destruct button", could go off at any time and destroy us without warning.

Reference: (https://youtube.com/watch?v=ijFm6DxNVyI)

59.

After vocalist Chris Cornell committed suicide, Linkin Park's Chester Bennington performed "Hallelujah" at his funeral. Two months later, following Bennington's death, Cornell's twelve-year-old daughter, who was also Bennington's goddaughter, performed "Hallelujah" as a tribute to the both of them.

Reference:(https://en.wikipedia.org/wiki/Linkin_Park#2015%E2%80%93present:_One_More_Light_and_Bennington's_death)

60.

The two women from the cast of "Rashomon" are still alive: one is 94 years old, and the other is 106.

Reference: (https://en.wikipedia.org/wiki/Rashomon#Cast)

61.

The Monroe Doctrine didn't just oppose European interference in the Western Hemisphere, it was also a promise the U.S. would not interfere in Europe.

Reference: (https://en.wikipedia.org/wiki/Monroe_Doctrine)

62.

The logo of Xbox is green colored because that was the marker pen that designer Horace Luke had at the moment.

Reference: (https://www.destructoid.com/the-origin-story-of-the-xbox-s-green-branding-295553.phtml)

63.

Shel Silverstein wrote a song called "Get My Rocks Off", as performed by Dr. Hook and the Medicine Show.

Reference: (http://repertoire.bmi.com)

64.

Legendary American general Douglas McArthur did not set foot on the U.S. mainland for 14 consecutive years. He left in 1937 to be a military advisor to the Philippine military. He returned in 1951, after being removed as supreme commander of UN forces in the Korean War.

Reference: (https://wikipedia.org/wiki/Douglas_MacArthur#Later_life)

65.

In 1877, an informal, unwritten deal sent Rutherford B. Hayes to the U.S. Presidency instead of Samuel Tilden, who had actually won the popular vote. In exchange, reconstruction collapsed and it would be another 75 years until Congress seriously considered civil rights again.

Reference: (https://learning.blogs.nytimes.com/2012/03/02/march-2-1877-rutherford-b-hayes-declared-winner-over-samuel-tilden-in-disputed-presidential-election/)

66.

Samuel L. Jackson and Christopher Lee had the same stunt double in "Star Wars: Episode III." His name is Kyle Rowling, and he also portrayed General Grievous in the same movie.

Reference: (https://www.youtube.com/watch?v=XffU0E5USxs)

67.

The inventor of petroleum jelly ate a spoonful every day, claiming it had tremendous health benefits. He lived to be 96. He also, reportedly, during a serious bout of pleurisy in his mid-1950s, had his nurse rub him from head to foot with the substance. He soon recovered.

Reference: (https://en.wikipedia.org/wiki/Robert_Chesebrough)

68.

The fictional company Dunder Mifflin from "The Office" became a real life member of the Scranton Chamber of Commerce. The town receives massive exposure as many businesses and locations are mentioned in the show.

Reference: (https://www.huffingtonpost.ca/entry/the-office-trivia_n_6004486)

69.

In the Villa Diodati, in 1816, during "the year without summer," Lord Byron, his doctor John Polidori, poet Percy Shelley and his teen bride Mary Shelley spent a rainy weekend writing horror stories. Mary would write "Frankenstein" and Polidori, "The Vampyre."

Reference: (https://en.wikipedia.org/wiki/Villa_Diodati)

70.

There have been several reported cases of people dying from laughter, including Greek philosopher Chrysippus, who died from laughing too hard at his own joke about a donkey eating figs and drinking wine.

Reference: (http://allthatsinteresting.com/death-from-laughter-chrysippus)

71.

Japan stunned the world in 1905 by handily defeating the much larger Russia Empire and winning significant concessions via the Treat of Portsmouth, which was mediated by President Roosevelt.

Reference: (https://en.wikipedia.org/wiki/Russo-Japanese_War)

72.

Peter Laird, co-creator of Teenage Mutant Ninja Turtles, hated the female turtle "Venus de Milo" from the live action TV show so much that when the 2007 Teenage Mutant Ninja Turtle movie was being made, one of his rules for director Kevin Munroe was that there was absolutely no mention of the character in the film.

Reference: (https://en.wikipedia.org/wiki/Ninja_Turtles:_The_Next_Mutation#Venus_de_Milo)

73.

Hyder, Alaska, is a town on the Southeastern most part of Alaska that functions as if it is a part of Canada. They use the Canadian Dollar and take off the same holidays as Canadians. They use British Columbian time.

Reference: (https://www.cntraveler.com/stories/2013-09-09/hyder-alaska-maphead-ken-jennings)

74.

There is a Popeye's episode spoofing "Star Wars: A New Hope", featuring Popeye as Luke, Olive as Leia, Wimpy as Han and Pluto as Darth Vader.

Reference: (https://www.youtube.com/watch?v=xhf11AoVt2I)

75.

False and unrealistic depictions of organ donation in primetime television shows, such as "Grey's Anatomy" and "House," causes people to refuse to register as organ donors.

Reference: (https://commons.pacificu.edu/cgi/viewcontent.cgi?article=1630&context=pa)

76.

President Andrew Johnson's disastrous 1866 "Swing Around the Circle" speaking tour, in which a stage collapsed, sent hundreds tumbling into a canal. Johnson then repeatedly compared himself to Jesus Christ while asking "Who has suffered more for the Union than I?"

Reference: (https://en.wikipedia.org/wiki/Swing_Around_the_Circle)

77.

The Dalai Lama is a Marxist.

Reference: (https://youtu.be/DhvlnC-oKEw)

78.

The earliest bicycles were velocipedes; bicycles on which you would propel yourself forward by pushing yourself from the ground with your feet.

Reference: (https://en.wikipedia.org/wiki/History_of_the_bicycle?repost)

79.

Cole Hamels, Texas Rangers pitcher, and his wife Heidi, donated their 32,000 square foot mega-mansion and 100 acres of land to a charity organization that helps children with special needs and chronic illnesses.

Reference: (https://www.nbcsports.com/philadelphia/the700level/cole-hamels-donates-millions-charity)

80.

The terminal building of Almaty International Airport, Kazakhstan burned down in just a few hours due to a fire started in the shashlik kitchen.

Reference: (https://en.wikipedia.org/wiki/Almaty_International_Airport)

81.

An increasing number of airports, especially in Europe, are taking on a "silent airport" philosophy. Nobody's going to call you to your flight, as announcements in all terminals will be made only in exceptional emergency circumstances.

Reference: (https://www.cnn.com/travel/article/silent-airports/index.html)

82.

The French Revolution's debate over how much power King Louis XVI had sparked the division of left and right in politics. Liberals and progressives on the left with traditionals on the right side of the house.

Reference: (https://www.history.com/news/election-101-how-did-the-political-labels-left-wing-and-right-wing-originate)

83.

The world's tallest sand castle was built in 1985 in St. Petersburg, Florida. It took 4,000 tons of sand, 12 workers, and 500 volunteers to complete. The end result was 37 feet tall.

Reference: (http://www.floridahistorynetwork.com/april-28-1985---worlds-tallest-sand-sculpture-built-at-treasure-island.html)

84.

To celebrate 25 years of Booker Prizes, there was a competition to select the best winner of the prize called "Booker of Bookers". It was done again 40 years later to award "The Best of Booker". "Midnight's Children" by Salman Rushdie won both of the times.

Reference: (https://en.wikipedia.org/wiki/The_Best_of_the_Booker)

85.

The Bagam or Eghap script is a partially deciphered Cameroonian script of several hundred characters. It was invented by King Pufong of the Bagam people, circa 1900, and used for letters and records, though it was never in wide use.

Reference: (https://en.wikipedia.org/wiki/Bagam_script)

86.

Kitty Genovese was murdered in 1964 around an apparent 37 witnesses who stood by and didn't act. One criticism was the lack of a recognizable emergency number, which is when 911 was born.

Reference: (https://www.wnyc.org/story/kitty-genovese/)

87.

Provideniya, Russia, is very close to the International Date Line. It has the closest Russian airport to the United States and tourism from nearby Alaska has given the local economy a significant boost.

Reference: (https://en.wikipedia.org/wiki/Provideniya)

88.

Vancouver, Canada, has the highest number of people of Asian descent outside of Asia than any other city.

Reference: (http://vancouversun.com/life/vancouver-is-most-asian-city-outside-asia-what-are-the-ramifications)

89.

The second officer of the Titanic stayed onboard till the end and was trapped underwater until a boiler explosion set him free. Later, he volunteered in World War II and helped evacuate over 120 men from Dunkirk.

Reference: (https://www.encyclopedia-titanica.org/titanic-survivor/charles-herbert-lightoller.html)

90.

George Washington signed the Tariff Act of 1789, making it the Republic's second ever piece of legislation. Increasing the domestic supply of manufactured goods, particularly war materials, was seen as an issue of national security.

Reference: (https://en.wikipedia.org/wiki/Tariff)

91.

The last fluent speaker of Ngarrindjer died in 1960s in South Australia, but recent attempts to revive the language include the release of an Ngarrindjeri dictionary in 2009. The 1864 Narrinyeri Bible was the first time portions of the Bible were translated into an Aboriginal language.

Reference: (https://en.wikipedia.org/wiki/Ngarrindjeri_language)

92.

Quentin Tarantino was on "The Golden Girls" as an Elvis impersonator.

Reference: (https://www.youtube.com/watch?v=_gD2hRpSg8U)

93.

The Canadian flag is only 54 years old.

Reference: (https://en.wikipedia.org/wiki/Flag_of_Canada)

94.

The largest mass lynching in America was against Sicilian Italians in New Orleans on March 14th, 1891. 11 Italians were hanged.

Reference: (http://www.knowlouisiana.org/entry/sicilian-lynchings-in-new-orleans)

95.

The land bridge between England and the rest of Continental Europe was rather large and called "Doggerland". It existed until about 6000 BC and was inhabited by many humans and Ice Age creatures.

Reference: (https://en.wikipedia.org/wiki/Doggerland)

96.

Gwaii Haanas National Park Reserve of Canada contains a village site of the Haida people. It features the largest collection of Haida totem poles in their original locations, and they are being allowed to succumb to natural decay in the lush temperate rainforest climate.

Reference: (https://en.wikipedia.org/wiki/Ninstints)

97.

Robert Plant once donated $10,000 to KBOO, a non-profit community radio station in Portland Oregon, to never play "Stairway to Heaven" ever again.

Reference: (https://en.wikipedia.org/wiki/KBOO#Stairway_to_Heaven)

98.

Peace Arch State Park is an international park between the U.S. and Canada. Visitors do not require either a passport or visa to pass through their applicable border crossing so long as they stay within the boundaries of the park and leave the park into the country from which they entered the park.

Reference: (https://en.wikipedia.org/wiki/Peace_Arch)

99.

There is sufficient evidence in humans for the carcinogenicity of alcohol consumption.

Reference: (http://monographs.iarc.fr/ENG/Monographs/vol100E/mono100E-11.pdf)

100.

During the battle of Arnhem, after numerous communication failures, a pigeon named William of Orange flew over 400 kilometers, or 250 miles, for over 4 and a half hours to deliver a message that would end up saving the lives of more than 2000 men. He later earned the Dickins Medal.

Reference: (https://en.wikipedia.org/wiki/William_of_Orange_%28pigeon%29)

101.

The highest recorded G Force experienced by a human being that lived was 214 G's during a crash in an Indycar Race in 2003.

Reference: (https://en.wikipedia.org/wiki/G-force#Horizontal)

102.

Some birds are capable of forming complex sentences as part of their own language; the first non-human creature ever known to do so.

Reference: (https://www.telegraph.co.uk/news/science/science-news/12187999/Birds-use-language-like-humans-joining-calls-together-to-form-sentences.html)

103.

The NSA was caught spying on the communications of the EU Commission, Council and Parliament in 2014.

Reference: (https://interc.pt/1zl45yE)

104.

Ketchup's originally a savory fish sauce that did not contain either sugar or tomatoes.

Reference: (https://en.wikipedia.org/wiki/Garum)

105.

Oskar Speck was a German man who paddled by folding kayak from Germany to Australia from 1932 to 1939 only to be arrested as a prisoner of war upon arrival.

Reference: (https://en.wikipedia.org/wiki/Oskar_Speck)

106.

The actual Everlasting Gobstopper "prop" used in the Gene Wilder movie was sold for $100,000 to the owners of TV show "Pawn Stars."

Reference: (https://en.wikipedia.org/wiki/Everlasting_Gobstopper)

107.

The "Jeopardy!" theme song is called "Think!" and was written by the show's creator, Merv Griffin, as a lullaby for his son.

Reference: (https://en.wikipedia.org/wiki/Jeopardy!#Theme_music)

108.

The Dyatlov Pass Incident is the mysterious unsolved death of 9 hikers who tore through their tents naked in sub-0 temperatures. 7 died of hypothermia, one of a fractured skull, one female team member had her tongue and eyes missing. The official cause of death was "unknown compelling force."

Reference: (https://en.wikipedia.org/w/index.php?title=Dyatlov_Pass_incident&)

109.

The largest number of deaths for females in the U.K. are expected to occur at age 88.9 years.

Reference:(https://www.ons.gov.uk/peoplepopulationandcommunity/healthandsocialcare/healthandlifeexpectancies/bulletins/healthstatelifeexpectanciesuk/2014to2016)

110.

In 2015, a Texas reptile enthusiast committed suicide by allowing a cobra to bite him.

Reference: (https://www.usatoday.com/story/news/nation-now/2015/11/12/teens-death-ruled-suicide-snakebite/75680504/)

111.

Game of Thrones has been the most-pirated TV series since 2012 and a single unnamed episode was downloaded about 4,280,000 times.

Reference: (https://en.wikipedia.org/wiki/Game_of_Thrones#availability)

112.

British celebrity chef Keith Floyd was cremated in a coffin made from banana leaves.

Reference: (https://en.wikipedia.org/wiki/Keith_Floyd)

113.

Britain's ghost trains are rare train services in the U.K. which only see a couple of passengers every day. They're only there because closing lines and stations is difficult and costly, and rail companies would rather run infrequent services than go through the cumbersome process.

Reference: (http://www.bbc.com/future/story/20150723-why-britain-has-secret-ghost-trains)

114.

In 1917, you could order a belt-fed machine gun from a Sears catalog.

Reference: (http://www.gutenberg.org/ebooks/54213?msg=welcome_stranger)

115.

Warner Bro's originally had an idea to cast Leonardo DiCaprio to star in Christopher Nolan's "The Dark Knight Rises" as the Riddler.

Reference: (http://wegotthiscovered.com/movies/leonardo-dicaprio-the-dark-knight-rises/)

116.

Zombies, as we know them, were inspired by Richard Matheson's 1954 novel "I Am Legend." George A. Romero's seminal film "Night of the Living Dead," was partly inspired by Matheson's novel.

Reference: (https://en.wikipedia.org/wiki/Zombie)

117.

The film "Happy Feet" originally had a large subplot regarding extraterrestrial space aliens; this wasn't cut until the final year of production.

Reference: (https://en.wikipedia.org/wiki/Happy_Feet#Production)

118.

The Lincoln canes were made in 1864 and delivered to the 19 Pueblos of New Mexico to mark the arrival of their United States Land Patents. Since then, the pueblos have used the Lincoln canes as the symbol of the pueblo governor's authority, even though differences in status do not exist.

Reference:(https://www.researchgate.net/publication/265047474_Symbolism_and_Significance_of_the_Lincoln_Canes_for_the_Pueblos_of_New_Mexico)

119.

Omar Bradly was promoted to the rank of General of the Army, 5 star general, after becoming the first Chairman of the Joint Chiefs of Staff so that Douglas MacArthur would not outrank him.

Reference: (https://en.wikipedia.org/wiki/Chairman_of_the_Joint_Chiefs_of_Staff)

120.

The first author known by name was a woman, Enheduanna of Ur.

Reference: (https://www.ancient.eu/Enheduanna/)

121.

Sean Connery's first job was as a milkman. Following his discharge from the Royal Navy he worked several jobs, including lifeguard, nude model, and coffin polisher.

Reference: (https://en.wikipedia.org/wiki/Sean_Connery#Early_life)

122.

Anna Bågenholm experienced one of the most extreme case of hypothermia ever recorded. Despite being dead for basically 40 minutes, doctors began performing CPR after her rescue and she revived with no brain damages thanks to the low temperature of her body.

Reference: (https://en.wikipedia.org/wiki/Anna_B%C3%A5genholm)

123.

Lou Gehrig's 2,130 consecutive games streak was helped out by then-Yankees GM Ed Barrow, who once called a rainout despite no rain while Gehrig was home with the flu. During the same streak, he was also knocked unconscious when hit by a pitch above the eye, but he still played the next day.

Reference: (https://nypost.com/2010/02/28/the-baseball-codes/)

124.

In the film "Terminator 2: Judgement Day," Arnold Schwarzenegger's famous line, "Hasta la vista, baby", is dubbed in the European Spanish version as "Sayonara, baby".

Reference: (https://en.wikipedia.org/wiki/Hasta_la_vista,_baby)

125.

Silica gel beads are non-toxic and should be kept out of reach of dogs and children for choking hazard.

Reference: (https://en.wikipedia.org/wiki/Silica_gel)

126.

30 years after the Berlin Wall fell, the town of Mödlareuth in Germany is still divided between East and West, with 2 mayors.

Reference: (https://www.warhistoryonline.com/war-articles/german-town-still-divided-30-years.html)

127.

In 1994, Crayola introduced the "new car" crayon. It was part of the "magic scent" collection and actually smelled liked a new car.

Reference: (https://www.complex.com/style/2013/06/the-best-crayola-crayon-colors/new-car)

128.

The little gaps perpendicular to the screw threads on plastic bottles are there for a reason, to allow gas to escape when you open the bottle so that it doesn't pop like a champagne bottle.

Reference: (https://www.youtube.com/watch?v=KL6k_rzRqfA)

129.

The 1983 recipient for the Mackay Trophy went to the crew of a KC-135 that "towed" a malfunctioning F-4 Phantom 160 miles. The tanker had to refuel said Phantom that had to fly at 45 degrees nose up for 160 miles until they could reach Gander, Newfoundland.

Reference: (https://tacairnet.com/2014/10/21/north-star-how-a-kc-135-crew-saved-an-f-4-phantom-over-the-atlantic/)

130.

Although the Maya were already in decay when the Spanish arrived and therefore did not offer much resistance, the location of their civilization centers in the deep jungle made their last city survive until 1697.

Reference: (https://en.wikipedia.org/wiki/Nojpet%C3%A9n)

131.

A section of passenger railroad in Alaska is called the Hurricane Turn. Rather than making scheduled station stops, it operates as a flag-stop meaning passengers in this remote area can simply wave the train down to stop. It's one of the last true flag-stop trains in the U.S.

Reference: (https://en.wikipedia.org/wiki/Hurricane_Turn)

132.

Marshmallows were originally made from the mallow plant, which grows in marshes.

Reference: (https://www.candyusa.com/candy-types/marshmallows/)

133.

Only three NBA players have become NBA referees after their playing careers ended.

Reference: (http://wearebasket.net/nba-players-became-referees/)

134.

Gold's color and low reactivity stem from relativistic effects exhibited by its s and p orbitals. Their electrons travel near the speed of light, increasing their mass and contracting their orbit while the d and f orbitals expand, absorbing blue light and reflecting yellow light back.

Reference: (http://web.uvic.ca/~chem426/relativity.pdf)

135.

The first swimming pool ever to go to sea had been installed on Titanic's sister ship, Olympic, which set sail a year before the Titanic.

Reference: (http://titanic.nmni.com/On-Board/Activities-on-board/1st-Class-Swimming-Pool.html)

136.

Family-owned and run builders, Richard Durtnell & Sons, is one of the oldest ongoing firms in the U.K. The first home they started building was for their family in 1591 and it is still standing, having been maintained, and restored after the World War II bombing, by generations of builders.

Reference: (http://www.kent-life.co.uk/out-about/places/thicker-than-mortar-1-1633948)

137.

One of the highest-grossing movies of 2011 was "The Lion King." Disney re-released it in 3D and it made $94 million that year.

Reference: (http://www.boxofficemojo.com/yearly/chart/?yr=2011)

138.

Early Judaism in the Levant had elements of polytheism. Wherein there's archeological findings of Yahweh having a wife.

Reference: (https://en.wikipedia.org/wiki/Asherah#In_Israel_and_Judah)

139.

When Claudius Galen wished to be chosen as physician to the High Priest of Asia's gladiators, he eviscerated an ape and challenged other physicians to repair the damage. When they refused, he performed surgery himself and won the High Priest's favor.

Reference: (https://en.wikipedia.org/wiki/Galen)

140.

Eric Lomax, a British ex-prisoner of war, was captured in 1942 by Japanese forces. Many years after the war, he tracked down the Japanese man who had tortured him, and forgave him.

Reference: (http://www.latimes.com/local/obituaries/la-me-eric-lomax-20121015-story.html)

141.

Neither John Denver, nor the writers of "Take Me Home, Country Road", had ever been to West Virginia. The road that inspired the song is actually in Maryland, and the landmarks mentioned in the lyrics more aptly describe the western region of Virginia.

Reference: (https://en.wikipedia.org/wiki/Take_Me_Home,_Country_Roads#Composition)

142.

Many Estonians speak Finnish since they grew up watching Finnish television broadcasts that were inadvertently transmitted over the Gulf of Finland acting as a window to the democratic west during Soviet occupation.

Reference:(https://www.researchgate.net/publication/301695738_Memories_of_Watching_Finnish_Television_in_Estonia_during_Soviet_Occupation)

143.

"Showgirls" holds 8 box office records for NC-17 movies.

Reference: (http://www.boxofficemojo.com/movies/?id=showgirls.htm)

144.

A Japanese sweet snack called "English toast", is neither English nor toast. It consists of two slices of white bread, covered with a layer of margarine, sprinkled with sugar and put together.

Reference: (https://soranews24.com/2014/11/22/japanese-netizens-show-love-for-english-toast-which-is-neither-english-nor-toast/)

145.

Paul Erdős would offer money for solutions to mathematical problems. The offers remained active despite his death. Solvers can either get an original check signed by Erdős or a cashable check from Ronald Graham, who is the administrator of solutions.

Reference: (https://en.wikipedia.org/wiki/Paul_Erd%C5%91s#Erd%C5%91s's_problems)

146.

Carey McWilliams became the first blind person to acquire a concealed weapons permit to allow him to carry a firearm for self-defense.

Reference: (https://en.wikipedia.org/wiki/Carey_McWilliams_(marksman))

147.

Maple syrup grades refers to the color of the syrup, not to its quality.

Reference: (http://deepmountainmaple.com/maple-facts-and-fictions)

148.

Virgin dogs can become quite distressed at finding themselves unable to separate during their first copulation, and may try to pull away or run.

Reference: (https://en.wikipedia.org/wiki/Canine_reproduction#Copulation)

149.

U.S. President Grover Cleveland's wife was the youngest First Lady, the first to be married in the White House, and the first to give birth while her husband was president. Grover met her shortly after she was born, when he was 27.

Reference: (https://en.wikipedia.org/wiki/Frances_Folsom_Cleveland_Preston)

150.

The original formula of Gripe Water, a non-prescription product sold in many countries around the world to relieve colic and other gastrointestinal ailments and discomforts of infants, contained alcohol, sodium bicarbonate, sugar, dill oil, and water.

Reference: (https://en.wikipedia.org/wiki/Gripe_water)

151.

An African midge is capable of anhydrobiosis, which is survival after losing 97% of its body water. They can also survive extreme temperatures from 90°C to -270°C, vacuums and high doses of radiation, and have the ability to make structural repairs to their DNA after rehydration.

Reference: (https://en.wikipedia.org/wiki/Polypedilum_vanderplanki)

152.

There is a temple in India where approximately 25,000 black rats live and are revered. Eating the food that has been nibbled on by the rats is considered to be a "high honor" and few white rats among the black rats are considered especially holy.

Reference: (https://en.wikipedia.org/wiki/Karni_Mata_Temple)

153.

In 1998, people would have gone to the movies and paid the full ticket price, only to see the "Star Wars (Episode I): The Phantom Menace" trailer, and leave.

Reference: (http://www.dorkly.com/post/70899/this-was-the-reaction-to-the-phantom-menace-trailer-debut-in-1998)

154.

Hans-Gunnar Liljenwall, a Swedish modern pentathlete, was the first athlete to ever be disqualified for doping in the Olympics. He drank "two beers" to calm his nerves before pistol shooting, giving him an unfair advantage.

Reference: (https://sok.se/idrottare/idrottare/h/hans-gunnar-liljenvall.html)

155.

Dinosaur names like "Triceratops", "Stegosaurus" and "Velociraptor" are just the name of the Genus they belong to, and the actual species' names are "Triceratops prorsus", "Stegosaurus stenops" and "Velociraptor mongoliensis".

Reference: (https://en.wikipedia.org/wiki/List_of_dinosaur_genera)

156.

The Omega Point is a scientific speculation that everything in the universe is fated to spiral towards a final point of divine unification.

Reference: (https://en.wikipedia.org/wiki/Omega_Point)

157.

Turkish people used salep in their ice cream, which makes it stickier than the ice-cream that most people are familiar with.

Reference: (https://en.wikipedia.org/wiki/Dondurma)

158.

Van Morrison once recorded an album for the sole purpose of getting out of a record contract. The album contained songs such as "Ring Worm", which is basically about letting someone know that they have ring worm.

Reference: (https://tonedeaf.com.au/7-of-the-nastiest-examples-of-revenge-musical-history/)

159.

The oldest unsolved problem in mathematics is proving whether or not odd perfect numbers exist. Mathematicians have been trying to solve this problem for 2,300 years.

Reference: (http://www.math.harvard.edu/~knill/seminars/perfect/handout.pdf)

160.

There are not one, but two former Soviet aircraft carriers being used as floating hotels and theme parks in China.

Reference: (https://en.wikipedia.org/wiki/Chinese_aircraft_carrier_Liaoning#Sale)

161.

The Imperial House of Japan is the oldest continuous hereditary monarchy in the world. Some sources indicate that it existed as far back as 660 BCE.

Reference: (https://en.wikipedia.org/wiki/Imperial_House_of_Japan)

162.

Soldiers of the 160th Special Forces pioneered the Army's nighttime flying techniques. The unit became known as the "Night Stalkers" because of its capability to strike undetected during the hours of darkness, and its unprecedented combat successes.

Reference: (https://www.military.com/special-operations/160th-special-operations-aviation-regiment.html)

163.

The Supreme Court once ruled on whether a tomato is a fruit or vegetable.

Reference: (https://thetakeout.com/the-supreme-court-once-ruled-on-whether-a-tomato-is-a-f-1826265946)

164.

The Ndrangheta's, the most powerful mafia in Italy in the 1990's and 2000's, annual revenue was between $50 to $60 billion, which was approximately 3.5% of the GDP of Italy, or as much as PepsiCo brings in annually.

Reference: (https://en.wikipedia.org/wiki/%27Ndrangheta)

165.

A study found that chimps that fling feces are more intelligent than those that do not. The feces flinging chimps have more heightened development in the motor cortex, more connections between it and the Broca's area, and are better communicators in the group.

Reference: (https://phys.org/news/2011-11-poop-throwing-chimps-intelligence.html)

166.

The endangered "Jackass Penguin" is so named due to the donkey-like braying sound it makes.

Reference: (https://en.wikipedia.org/wiki/African_penguin)

167.

Microsoft purchased DOS from a company named Seattle Computer Products. The software was originally named "QDOS" or "Quick and Dirty Operating System."

Reference: (https://en.wikipedia.org/wiki/Seattle_Computer_Products)

168.

In Chinese traditional medicine, visible sclera beneath the iris means bodily imbalance. Upper sclera means mental imbalance. Stress and fatigue can also cause it. The state attracts accidents and violence.

Reference: (https://en.wikipedia.org/wiki/Sanpaku)

169.

There are more possible iterations of chess games than there are atoms in the observable universe.

Reference: (https://www.youtube.com/watch?v=Km024eldY1A&t=1s)

170.

An IMAX movie was the second highest domestic grossing film released in 1976.

Reference: (https://www.the-numbers.com/movie/To-Fly#tab=summary)

171.

In 1968, a Syrian Air Force pilot landed a Soviet-made MiG-17 fighter jet at an airstrip in northern Israel, mistakenly believing he was in Lebanon. Israel quickly loaned the plane to the U.S. Air Force, who tested and exploited it as part of a secret foreign aircraft evaluation program at Area 51.

Reference: (https://en.wikipedia.org/wiki/HAVE_DRILL)

172.

Former Steely Dan and Doobie Brothers guitarist Jeff Baxter is also a missile defense consultant for the United States government.

Reference: (https://en.wikipedia.org/wiki/Jeff_Baxter#Defense_consulting_career)

173.

The Mugwumps were political activists who bolted from the Republican Party by supporting Democratic candidate Grover Cleveland. They rejected James G. Blaine's financial corruption and switched parties. The Mugwumps swung New York state and the election.

Reference: (https://en.wikipedia.org/wiki/Mugwumps)

174.

Hydrangea is a genus of 70 to 75 species of flowering plants native to southern and eastern Asia and the Americas. By far the greatest species diversity is in eastern Asia, notably China, Japan, and Korea.

Reference: (https://wikipedia.org/wiki/Hydrangea)

175.

Viggo Mortensen speaks seven languages.

Reference: (https://youtu.be/IxtGp4R9Kw4)

176.

There was a recorded mutiny in space, which took place on Skylab during an endurance mission.

Reference: (https://www.smithsonianmag.com/smart-news/mutiny-space-why-these-skylab-astronauts-never-flew-again-180962023/)

177.

In some high schools, in Japan, the students need to hatch and raise chickens before killing and eating them.

Reference: (http://www.odditycentral.com/news/controversial-high-school-class-has-students-hatching-and-raising-chickens-before-killing-and-eating-them.html)

178.

Methemoglobinemia is a blood disorder which causes severe sufferers to have blue skin. People with the disorder have raised levels of methemoglobin, causing their blood to be brown, and in severe cases, their skin to have a blue hue.

Reference: (https://en.wikipedia.org/wiki/Methemoglobinemia)

179.

The first commercially packaged toilet paper was made in flat sheets medicated with aloe and was advertised as a treatment for hemorrhoids.

Reference: (http://www.toiletpaperhistory.net/toilet-paper-history/history-of-toilet-paper/)

180.

The old St. Paul's Cathedral in London was 100 feet taller than the current one.

Reference: (https://en.wikipedia.org/wiki/List_of_tallest_church_buildings)

181.

Patrick Bertoletti once drank a 22 ounce 7-11 Slurpee in 9 seconds. He also ate 275 pickled Jalapeños in 8 minutes and another time took down 72 cupcakes in 6 minutes.

Reference: (https://en.wikipedia.org/wiki/Patrick_Bertoletti)

182.

There was a professional football player named Glenn Frey who played for the Philadelphia Eagles in the 1930s, well before Glenn Frey, the singer, and the Eagles, the band, became famous.

Reference: (https://en.wikipedia.org/wiki/Glenn_Frey_(American_football))

183.

A group of audiophiles were unable to tell the difference between music transmitted over Monster cables versus a coat hanger.

Reference: (https://gizmodo.com/363154/audiophile-deathmatch-monster-cables-vs-a-coat-hanger)

184.

Shaggy was a Marine prior to his music career. He served with a Field Artillery Battery in the 10th Marine Regiment during the Persian Gulf War.

Reference: (https://en.wikipedia.org/wiki/Shaggy_(musician)#Military_career)

185.

There's a wrestling federation comprised only of dwarfs.

Reference: (https://www.microwrestling.com/)

186.

Although Smith remains the most common surname in America, for the first time two Hispanic names, Garcia and Rodriguez, have joined Smith, Johnson, and Miller in the top ten most common surnames in the nation.

Reference: (https://www.infoplease.com/us/miscellaneous/most-common-last-names)

187.

Viggo Mortensen purchased the horse he rode in "Lord of The Rings." The horse had a hard time adjusting to the lights and sounds on set and it took a while for them to get in sync. "We got through it together and became friends. I wanted to stay in touch with him," said Viggo.

Reference: (http://ca.ign.com/articles/2004/03/04/ign-inteviews-viggo-mortensen)

188.

The word "quarantine" comes from the Venetian form of the Italian quaranta giorni, meaning forty days. The people of Dubrovnik, imposed a 40-day isolation of ships and people off-port to prevent the Black Death from entering the city. Earlier in 1377, there was a "trentine" isolation-period of 30 days.

Reference: (https://en.wikipedia.org/wiki/Quarantine#History)

189.

The Batoro people of Uganda have a rite of passage called "kachapati", meaning "spraying the wall", where the older women of the village will teach the younger females how to ejaculate when they reach puberty.

Reference: (https://en.wikipedia.org/wiki/Female_ejaculation#Anthropological_accounts)

190.

Japanese people are offered extra incentives for surrendering their driver's license such as discounted funerals.

Reference: (https://www.bbc.com/news/amp/blogs-news-from-elsewhere-39327663)

191.

The Village People only did the Y in YMCA in their original music video.

Reference: (https://www.youtube.com/watch?v=Vc0gYbTNctU&feature=youtu.be)

192.

There is a city in Japan, whose 10% of the population is Brazilian. About 15% of the people there speaks Portuguese as their native language.

Reference: (https://en.wikipedia.org/wiki/%C5%8Cizumi,_Gunma)

193.

America has its own Stonehenge.

Reference: (https://en.wikipedia.org/wiki/America's_Stonehenge)

194.

Arizona started issuing licenses that were good until age 60. Starting at 65, drivers must renew every five years, with a vision test each time.

Reference: (https://www.dmv.org/az-arizona/renew-license.php)

195.

Sia wrote Rihanna's "Diamonds" in 14 minutes.

Reference: (http://www.digitalspy.com/music/news/a565956/sia-wrote-rihannas-diamonds-in-14-minutes/)

196.

10% of drinkers consume over 50% of the alcohol.

Reference: (https://www.soberlink.com/15-facts-alcoholism-part/)

197.

Picking up trash while out on a run or working out is called "plogging."

Reference: (https://www.citylab.com/life/2018/03/plogging-exercise-trash-running/554456/)

198.

Fleetwood Mac's "Dreams" was Stevie Nicks' way to break up with Lindsay Buckingham. Buckingham responded with "Go Your Own Way."

Reference: (http://www.inherownwords.com/dreams.htm)

199.

People with Capgras syndrome have an irrational belief that someone they know or recognize has been replaced by an imposter. Capgras syndrome is what's known as a delusional misidentification and is most commonly associated with Alzheimer's disease or dementia.

Reference: (https://www.healthline.com/health/capgras-syndrome)

200.

The Recycled Orchestra of Cateura creates instruments out of recycled materials found in the landfill of Cateura, Paraguay.

Reference: (https://www.npr.org/sections/deceptivecadence/2016/09/14/493794763/from-trash-to-triumph-the-recycled-orchestra)

201.

Archaeologists in South Africa have found the oldest painting that dates back over 164,000 years.

Reference: (https://www.smithsonianmag.com/history/journey-oldest-cave-paintings-world-180957685/)

202.

Followers of Glycon, a snake god worshiped in the Roman Empire, did not worship a statue or spirit of a snake, but an actual physical serpent that was allegedly a hand puppet. Comic book writer Alan Moore has declared himself a devotee of Glycon.

Reference: (https://en.wikipedia.org/wiki/Glycon)

203.

The Mohs scale is a mineral hardness scale that was officially created in 1812 by German geologist and mineralogist Friedrich Mohs, though based on a system that dates back to at least 300 BC.

Reference: (https://en.wikipedia.org/wiki/Mohs_scale_of_mineral_hardness)

204.

Goa music originated from a state called GOA in India.

Reference: (https://en.wikipedia.org/wiki/Goa_trance)

205.

The Regina Cyclone of 1912 remains the deadliest tornado in Canadian history with a total of 28 fatalities. The city forced those rendered homeless by the disaster to pay for the nightly use of cots set up in schools and city parks.

Reference: (https://en.wikipedia.org/wiki/Regina_Cyclone)

206.

Despite what Monty Python would have you believe, Spanish Inquisitions were expected, they would give a 30-day notice of their arrival.

Reference: (https://en.wikipedia.org/wiki/Spanish_Inquisition)

207.

Tom Petty was so popular that his record label wanted to charge $1 more for his 1981 album "Hard Promises" than the standard $8.98, but they backed down after he considered naming the album "$8.98."

Reference: (https://en.wikipedia.org/wiki/Hard_Promises)

208.

Maarten van der Weijden, a Dutch swimmer and leukemia survivor, swam across the English canal twice in one go.

Reference: (http://eindhovennews.com/news/2017/08/maarten-van-der-weijden-crosses-english-channel-twice/)

209.

1 drop of water is equal to .05 milliliters. A leaky faucet will drip 20,000 times to equal a liter or 90,921.8 times to equal a gallon.

Reference: (http://askascientist.co.uk/physics/many-drops-water/)

210.

$1000 bills, as well as other large denominations, exist in the U.S., and were actually used until they were taken out of circulation in 1969.

Reference: (https://en.wikipedia.org/wiki/Large_denominations_of_United_States_currency)

211.
There's huge wall with dinosaurs footprints in Bolivia.

Reference: (http://www.amusingplanet.com/2013/10/cal-orcko-300-feet-wall-with-over-5000.html?m=1)

212.
The Toynbee tiles are plates of an unknown origin scattered across two continents and containing cryptic references to "2001: A Space Odyssey."

Reference: (https://en.wikipedia.org/wiki/Toynbee_tiles)

213.
A 2003 study found evidence that Genghis Khan's DNA is present in about 16 million men alive today. However, an article from 2015 claims that ten other men left genetic legacies so huge they rival Genghis Khan's.

Reference: (https://www.smithsonianmag.com/smart-news/other-men-who-left-huge-genetic-legacies-likes-genghis-khan-180954052/)

214.
The Akan language of Ghana came to the Caribbean and South America. The descendants of escaped slaves in the interior of Suriname and the Maroons in Jamaica still use a form of this language, including Akan names.

Reference: (https://en.wikipedia.org/wiki/Akan_language)

215.
Mithridates VI was so paranoid of being poisoned that he slowly drank small amounts of it throughout his life in order to gain an immunity. When he was captured by the Romans, he tried to kill himself with poison but could not.

Reference: (https://en.wikipedia.org/wiki/Mithridates_VI_of_Pontus)

216.
There was a 4th Rice Krispie gnome named Pow.

Reference: (https://www.smithsonianmag.com/arts-culture/untold-tale-pow-fourth-rice-krispies-elf-180949379/)

217.

Wild oats and rye self-domesticated by growing in wheat fields, imitating wheat over generations, and being selected for by agriculture, a process called Vavilovian mimicry.

Reference: (https://en.wikipedia.org/wiki/Vavilovian_mimicry)

218.

Singer Million Stylez is half Japanese, half French, was born in Sweden, sings in Jamaican and his hit "Miss Fatty" was shot in Cuba and distributed by a German company.

Reference: (https://en.wikipedia.org/wiki/Million_Stylez)

219.

Pumpernickel bread is derived from the Baviarian word "pumpern", meaning flatulence, and "nickel", meaning goblin or devil, so it is "devil's fart" bread.

Reference: (https://en.wikipedia.org/wiki/Pumpernickel#Etymology)

220.

Sir Arthur Conan Doyle once solved a real-life mystery case and helped clear an innocent man of murder but he didn't pay Conan Doyle's legal fees even though he was awarded £6,000 in compensation.

Reference: (https://www.conandoyleinfo.com/life-conan-doyle/conan-doyles-own-mystery-cases/oscar-slater/)

221.

In 1806, a hen in Leeds, England, began laying eggs on which the phrase "Christ is coming" was written. Eventually it was discovered to be a hoax. The owner, Mary Bateman, had written on the eggs in a corrosive ink so as to etch the eggs, and reinserted the eggs back into the hen's oviduct.

Reference: (https://en.wikipedia.org/wiki/Mary_Bateman??)

222.

Our days of the week come from the names of Norse gods.

Reference: (http://vikings.mrdonn.org/daysoftheweek.html)

223.

Lucille "2" Austero from "Arrested Development" played by Liza Minnelli appeared on 2006 album My Chemical Romance's "The Black Parade," providing backing vocals and singing a solo part with Gerard Way on the track "Mama."

Reference: (https://www.rollingstone.com/music/features/gerard-way-20061214)

224.

Many famous and classic authors deny the intentional use of symbolism in their works.

Reference: (http://mentalfloss.com/article/30937/famous-novelists-symbolism-their-work-and-whether-it-was-intentional)

225.

In 1846, the life expectancy in Iceland was 18 years. Today it is 83 years.

Reference: (https://ourworldindata.org/grapher/life-expectancy?year=1846)

226.

J.R.R. Tolkien once received a goblet from a fan inscribed with "One Ring to Rule Them All..." inscribed on the rim in black speech. Tolkien never drank out of it, since it was written in an accursed language, and instead used it as an ashtray.

Reference: (https://en.wikipedia.org/wiki/Black_Speech)

227.

There are only 7 authors to hit number 1 on the New York Times Bestsellers list for both Fiction and Nonfiction, among them Hemingway, Steinbeck, Wallace and Jimmy Buffett.

Reference: (https://www.buffettnews.com/resources/personalfacts/)

228.

In 2003, unknown Russian mathematician Grigori Perelman proved the long awaited Poincaré conjecture publishing it openly. He is the only person to reject the Fields Medal, the Clay Millennium prize of $1,000,000 and the EMS prize. He has since vanished back to obscurity.

Reference: (https://www.youtube.com/watch?v=GItmC9lxeco)

229.

O'Connor v. Donaldson was a landmark decision in mental health law. It stated that those that are non-dangerous cannot be confined if they have help of friends and family.

Reference: (https://en.wikipedia.org/wiki/O'Connor_v._Donaldson)

230.

Khabarovsk, Russia, is only 30 kilometers from the Chinese border. Before 1860, this was a typical Chinese city, with more than 50% Han residents and it was once a regional capital during the Tang dynasty.

Reference: (https://en.wikipedia.org/wiki/Khabarovsk)

231.

Airplanes store fuel in their wings.

Reference: (https://www.an-aviation.com/why-is-fuel-stored-in-the-wings-of-aircraft/)

232.

Construction on the New York City Water Tunnel No. 3 began on the water supply system in 1970 and will be completed in 2020. The tunnel will be 60 miles long and 500 feet underground.

Reference: (https://en.wikipedia.org/wiki/New_York_City_Water_Tunnel_No._3)

233.

Kentucky produces 95% of the world's bourbon.

Reference: (https://kybourbon.com/bourbon_culture-2/key_bourbon_facts/)

234.

Donald Glover had a brief stint in the "Adventure Time" series as fan favorite Marshall Lee.

Reference: (https://www.youtube.com/watch?v=AATGCGy0sLc)

235.

Archie Karas, a Greek-American gambler, turned a $10,000 loan with 100% interest into $42 million by gambling between 1992 and 1995, only to lose it all in around a month.

Reference: (https://en.wikipedia.org/wiki/Archie_Karas)

236.

In 1998, the MGM Grand casino removed its "lion's mouth" entrance, as many Asian gamblers saw passing through a lion's mouth as a sign of bad luck.

Reference: (http://aarontodd.casinocitytimes.com/article/understanding-cultural-differences-33199)

237.

With the Guano Islands Act, you can claim any unclaimed island for the U.S. if it has bird feces on it.

Reference: (http://mentalfloss.com/article/66868/how-old-bird-poop-law-can-help-you-claim-island)

238.

Chance The Rapper donated over $2 million to Chicago Public Schools. Working with 20 principals and his non-profit SocialWorks, he helped the schools gain $100,000 over 3 years, and selected the schools based on budgetary and individual needs.

Reference: (http://abc7chicago.com/education/chance-the-rapper-raises-over-$2-million-for-20-cps-schools/2366046/)

239.

Michelle Urry was Playboy Magazine's cartoon editor for over 30 years. She got the job after making founder Hugh Hefner laugh. "The fact that I brought to it an inordinately dirty mind was my own doing," she said, "—I mean, I don't think he expected that kind of bonus."

Reference: (http://www.tcj.com/magazine-gag-cartoons-michelle-urry-and-cartooning-for-playboy/)

240.

The displaying of the Mona Lisa has caused its colors to become quite faded. A sister painting made by a student of Da Vinci at the same time was kept in storage and is much more vibrant.

Reference: (https://www.npr.org/2012/02/02/146288063/painting-sheds-new-light-on-the-mona-lisa)

241.

Queen Elizabeth II is a descendant of the founder of Islam, the Prophet Muhammad.

Reference: (https://observer.news/world/study-reveals-queen-elizabeth-ii-descendant-prophet-muhammad/)

242.

The Vatican Secret Archives contain documents such as a handwritten transcript of the trial against Galileo, a letter from Mary Queen of Scots from when she was awaiting execution, and a letter from Michelangelo complaining about not being paid for his work in the Sistine Chapel.

Reference: (https://en.wikipedia.org/wiki/Vatican_Secret_Archives)

243.

A fully automated trans-Atlantic flight, including automatic takeoff and landing, was completed in 1947.

Reference: (https://www.flightglobal.com/pdfarchive/view/1947/1947%20-%201745.html)

244.

Prince Harry served in the military for 10 years, became a captain and undertook 2 tours in Afghanistan.

Reference: (https://www.royal.uk/prince-harrys-military-career)

245.

While he often said "my dear Watson" and "elementary", Sherlock Holmes never actually said the often used quote, "Elementary, my dear Watson".

Reference: (http://sherlockholmesquotes.com/elementary-my-dear-watson/)

246.

By the time he was 16, Warren Buffet had made $53,000.

Reference: (https://amp.businessinsider.com/facts-about-warren-buffett-2016-12)

247.

There is a massive 112,000 square foot bunker built under the luxury Greenbriar Hotel in West Virginia designed to house the United States Congress, 100 senators, 435 congressmen and about 500 staffers, in the aftermath of a thermonuclear apocalypse.

Reference: (http://www.historynet.com/secret-doomsday-bunker.htm)

248.

In 2011, a man in China accidentally buried his friend alive and got 2 years in prison for criminal negligence.

Reference: (https://en.wikipedia.org/wiki/Suicide_in_China#Legality)

249.

For a better chance to survive in a falling elevator you should it or lay down so the impact can be distributed over your entire body. Jumping is not the obvious choice. The inertia may cause you to hit your head on the top of it.

Reference: (https://hypescience.com/queda-elevador-sobreviver/)

250.

Ottomans had plans to invade eastern Armenia and continue their genocide there in May 1918, however, thanks to the ferocious defense of 9.000 Armenians, the invasion was repelled and Ottomans were forced to recognize Armenia as an independent nation.

Reference: (https://en.wikipedia.org/wiki/Battle_of_Sardarabad)

251.

There is a Gary Gygax memorial where people ask to have their dice blessed by the spirit of the man who created Dungeons and Dragons.

Reference: (https://www.roadsideamerica.com/tip/54341)

252.

Benedict Cumberbatch was kidnapped at gunpoint in South Africa. He talked his way out of being killed and said, "It taught me that you come into this world as you leave it, on your own. It's made me want to live a life slightly less ordinary."

Reference: (https://www.telegraph.co.uk/culture/tvandradio/9009080/Sherlock-star-Benedict-Cumberbatch-survived-kidnap-attempt-in-South-Africa.html)

253.

Plato's real name was Aristocles, and Plato was a nickname he was given due to his broad stature.

Reference: (https://en.wikipedia.org/wiki/Plato#Name)

254.

When Queen Victoria first moved to Buckingham Palace, it was dirty and cold as staff were lax and lazy and chimneys smoked so much that fires were dampened down.

Reference: (http://blog.premiumtours.co.uk/buckingham-palace-facts/)

255.

The city of Dallas, Texas has lost every single one of 82 court cases against the same man, Robert Groden, over several decades.

Reference: (http://www.dallasobserver.com/news/dallas-has-now-lost-82-cases-against-robert-groden-someone-call-guinness-8680799)

256.

The Grumman LLV, the delivery vehicle most widely used by the USPS, is one of the only U.S. produced vehicles with the driver's seat on the right side of the vehicle, and averages only 10 miles per gallon in operation.

Reference: (https://en.wikipedia.org/wiki/Grumman_LLV)

257.

Clown Alleys are clubhouses for clowns. Their purpose is to continue the tradition of the American clown, holding workshops taught by older clowns and acting as a center for all of a clown's needs. Alleys appear in nearly every city across America, and in many smaller towns.

Reference: (http://thelittlerebellion.com/index.php/2017/12/clowns-a-misunderstood-and-declining-profession/)

258.

There is a form of debugging called rubber duck debugging, where you debug code by explaining it. The name is in reference to the book "The Pragmatic Programmer" where a programmer would debug code by explaining it, word by word, to his rubber duck.

Reference: (https://en.wikipedia.org/wiki/Rubber_duck_debugging)

259.

Manchester United changed kits at halftime when they were 3-0 down as players were having difficulty spotting each other in the "invisible" grey kit.

Reference: (http://www.skysports.com/football/news/11095/10775341/the-story-of-man-utds-half-time-kit-change-against-southampton)

260.

Chenonceau Castle in Loire Valley, France, was built between 1515 and 1521 by Thomas Bohier, overseen by his wife Katherine Briconnet.

Reference: (http://www.castles.francethisway.com/chateau-chenonceau.php)

261.

A Brazilian conman named Carlos Kaiser, became the best football and soccer player in Brazil, without ever kicking a ball nor having any professional football experience.

Reference: (https://www.fourfourtwo.com/features/confessions-carlos-kaiser-footballs-biggest-conman)

262.

As late as the 1970s, many Western countries had laws preventing married women from having jobs. This was commonly referred to as a marriage bar.

Reference: (https://www.wikipedia.org/wiki/Marriage_bar)

263.

The Toba Catastrophe is the theory that 75,000 years ago, a massive volcano eruption reduced the human population to 3000, causing a genetic bottleneck that has reduced the genetic diversity in humans today.

Reference: (https://en.wikipedia.org/wiki/Toba_catastrophe_theory#Genetic_bottleneck_theory)

264.

The comic book series of "Men in Black" that inspired the "Men in Black" trilogy was initially inspired by actual reports of real men in black.

Reference:(http://www.slate.com/blogs/browbeat/2012/05/23/men_in_black_sightings_do_they_still_happen_.html)

265.

The falling dominoes scene in "V for Vendetta" involved 22,000 dominoes assembled by four professional domino assemblers for the two day shoot.

Reference: (http://mentalfloss.com/article/75813/13-riotous-facts-about-v-vendetta)

266.

A Manx shearwater lived to at least 52. The average lifespan of sea birds is about 15 to 20 years.

Reference: (http://news.bbc.co.uk/1/hi/wales/north_west/2976141.stm)

267.

Bin Laden was taught by Jimmy Wu, a Taiwanese Judo coach, who was the coach for the Saudi national team.

Reference: (https://www.telegraph.co.uk/news/worldnews/al-qaeda/8500136/I-taught-judo-to-Osama-bin-Laden.html)

268.

Hampton, Florida, is a city that annexed 1,260 feet of U.S. 301 and used it to raise $211,328, earning it a reputation as a speed trap on a national level.

Reference: (https://wikipedia.org/wiki/Hampton,_Florida)

269.

In 2012, a study conducted by the Society of Chemical Industry, verified that you can use essential oils to ward off wasps.

Reference: (https://www.ncbi.nlm.nih.gov/pubmed/23081867)

270.

Thrill killing is murder that is motivated by the sheer excitement of the act.

Reference: (https://en.wikipedia.org/wiki/Thrill_killing/)

271.

Dolphins can understand human language syntax.

Reference: (http://dolcotec.org/background/earlier-language-work)

272.

From June 1948, the U.S. Air Force and the Royal Air Force flew 280.000 flights in 12 months to help the citizens of Berlin with coal and food during the Blockade of Berlin, a gesture of kindness after the cruelty of war.

Reference: (https://en.wikipedia.org/wiki/Berlin_Blockade#End_of_the_blockade)

273.

Snakes can see UV up to 1 meter in front of them.

Reference: (https://youtu.be/FXfrncRey-4)

274.

It's a custom in some Jewish circles to use an inverted T symbol (⊥) instead of a plus symbol (+) in mathematical contexts, because the plus symbol looks similar to a Christian cross.

Reference: (https://en.wikipedia.org/wiki/Plus_and_minus_signs#Alternative_plus_sign)

275.

In 1518, a "dancing plague" affected around 400 people in Strasbourg, Alsace. People who were affected danced for days without rest and some of them eventually succumbed to heart attack, stroke, or exhaustion.

Reference: (https://en.wikipedia.org/wiki/Dancing_plague_of_1518)

276.

The patron saint of the internet, programmers and computer users is Isodore of Seville.

Reference: (https://en.wikipedia.org/wiki/Isidore_of_Seville)

277.

Mice "whistle" to find a mate and define territory. They "whistle" by using a mechanism similar to that of a jet engine inside their throats.

Reference: (https://www.independent.ie/world-news/and-finally/mice-whistle-like-a-jet-engine-to-attract-a-mate-35121462.html)

278.

A "Kardashian" is an unofficial unit of measurement that denotes 72 days of marriage.

Reference: (http://awesci.com/10-fancy-units-of-measurement/)

279.

The Jain unit of measurement "Palyopama" is defined as the length of time it would take to empty a pit 8x8x8 miles tightly packed full of the hair of seven-day old babies if you were to remove 1/8th of each hair once every 100 years.

Reference: (https://en.wikipedia.org/wiki/Naraka_(Jainism)#Notes)

280.

Alexander the Great was as tall as Napoleon Bonaparte.

Reference: (http://www.pothos.org/content/indexdd72.html?page=body-and-height)

281.

At one time, there were 10 times more grape-flavored products than grapes grown. If all the real grapes were used on grape soda, there wouldn't be any left for wine.

Reference: (https://www.npr.org/sections/thesalt/2017/11/03/560048780/is-natural-flavor-healthier-than-artificial-flavor)

282.

Murrinh-patha, which literally translates to "language-good", is an Australian Aboriginal language spoken by over 2,500 people. At most, 11% of its vocabulary is shared with any other language it has been tested against.

Reference: (https://en.wikipedia.org/wiki/Murrinh-patha_language)

283.

Billiard tables are traditionally made with slate tops to give them their flat play surface.

Reference: (https://electronics.howstuffworks.com/billiard-table2.htm)

284.

Helen Keller helped found the ACLU.

Reference: (https://en.wikipedia.org/wiki/American_Civil_Liberties_Union)

285.

Picher, Oklahoma is a town that had to be abandoned after it was discovered that an old lead mine was poisoning the residents. The real nail in the coffin came when an F-4 tornado hit in 2008. Today, the town sits completely empty.

Reference: (http://5newsonline.com/2015/11/02/picher-oklahoma-the-biggest-environmental-disaster-youve-never-heard-of/)

286.

Iceland's armed police force is called the "Viking Squad."

Reference: (http://www.bbc.com/news/magazine-25201471)

287.

Coins have ridges in order to make it impossible to shave them down without the result being obvious. As a side benefit, the receded edges also made coin design more intricate and counterfeiting more difficult.

Reference: (https://www.history.com/news/why-do-coins-have-ridges)

288.

During the Cold War, the U.S. considered airdropping enormous condoms labeled "Medium" into USSR, to demoralize them against an anatomically superior American Army.

Reference: (http://mentalfloss.com/article/30880/11-things-you-didn%E2%80%99t-know-about-america%E2%80%99s-spymasters)

289.

With 20 official titles including 2 FIFA World Cups, 2 Olympic golds, and 15 Copa America wins, Uruguay holds the world record for most international titles held by any country.

Reference: (https://en.wikipedia.org/wiki/Uruguay_national_football_team)

290.

Patrick Dennis, after having written one of the most popular books of the 20th century, "Auntie Mame", became a butler to Roy Croc, founder of McDonalds, who had no idea of his previous fame.

Reference: (https://en.wikipedia.org/wiki/Patrick_Dennis)

291.

Elizabeth Bathory still holds 2 Guinness World Records for serial killers: most kills by a female and most by a Westerner.

Reference: (http://www.guinnessworldrecords.com/world-records/most-prolific-female-murderer)

292.

Butch Hartman, creator of "The Fairly Odd Parents" and "Danny Phantom," was the live action reference model for Kocoum and a few scenes of John Smith's in Disney's "Pocahontas."

Reference: (http://disney.wikia.com/wiki/Butch_Hartman)

293.

Henry Kissinger told the Thai foreign minister about Khmer Rouge and Pol Pot: "You should tell the Cambodians that we will be friends with them. They are murderous thugs but we won't let that stand in our way."

Reference:(https://en.wikipedia.org/wiki/Allegations_of_United_States_support_for_the_Khmer_Rouge#US_military_and_diplomatic_support)

294.

In 2016, Kanye West was busted pirating editing software from torrent site Pirate Bay.

Reference: (https://www.popularmechanics.com/culture/music/a19714/kanye-busted-torrenting-editing-software-from-the-pirate-bay/)

295.

Valdosta State University administratively withdrew a student for peacefully protesting the construction of new campus parking garages, resulting in a civil rights lawsuit and a $900,000 payout.

Reference: (https://en.wikipedia.org/wiki/Hayden_Barnes_controversy)

296.

The Overjustification Effect is an effect where monetary gains or prizes decreases motivation to perform a task.

Reference: (https://en.wikipedia.org/wiki/Overjustification_effect)

297.

Two male bears from a zoo in Croatia were caught engaging in oral sex. Oral sex is well documented in mammals as diverse as rats, fruit bats, horses, goats, dolphins, most primates, cheetahs, lions, hyenas, sheep and cattle.

Reference: (https://sciencing.com/animals-besides-humans-mate-pleasure-8390317.html)

298.

The Arlington Ladies are a group of volunteers that attend funeral services at Arlington National Cemetery to ensure that no soldier, sailor, airman or coast guardsman is buried alone.

Reference: (https://www.arlingtoncemetery.mil/Funerals/About-Funerals/Arlington-Ladies)

299.

The football huddle was invented during the 1890's by the quarterback of the all deaf Gallaudet College football team so that the players from the opposing teams wouldn't be able to read the plays as they were signing them to each other.

Reference: (https://theweek.com/articles/451763/true-origin-story-football-huddle)

300.

Men and women on average give directions differently. Women will describe directions using landmarks and left or right turns, whereas men will use cardinal directions and distance information.

Reference: (https://www.ncbi.nlm.nih.gov/pubmed/14607168)

301.

A species of waxworm has been shown to be capable of digesting plastics. This discovery may eventually lead to the isolation of an enzyme that can be sprayed on plastic to encourage them to degrade rapidly into more ecologically friendly materials.

Reference: (https://hydrationanywhere.com/tiny-plastic-eating-caterpillars-hold-answer-trash-problem/)

302.

The Irish Air Corps used crashed enemy aircraft to expand their air force during World War II.

Reference: (https://en.wikipedia.org/wiki/Irish_Air_Corps)

303.

"Death by misadventure" is an official coroner's term that attributes an accident that occurred due to a dangerous risk that was taken voluntarily.

Reference: (https://en.wikipedia.org/wiki/Death_by_misadventure)

304.

There's an orangutan at the San Diego Zoo that likes to sneak out of his cage at night and wander the park, then sneak back in the morning.

Reference: (http://www.bbc.co.uk/newsbeat/article/40959970/this-is-what-animals-have-done-when-they-escaped-from-captivity)

305.

Buddhahood is the state of an enlightened being, who having found the path of cessation of suffering, is in the state of "No-more-Learning".

Reference: (https://en.wikipedia.org/wiki/Buddhahood#Explanation_of_the_term_Buddha)

306.

For 1 billion euros, Austria built a fully functional nuclear reactor in 1978, but it was never turned on.

Reference: (http://www.nuclear-power-plant.net/index.php?lang=en&item=history)

307.

Rosa Parks wasn't the first African American to defy authority on public transportation. On July 16th, 1865, Elizabeth Jennings boarded and refused to leave a whites only horse drawn streetcar.

Reference: (https://en.wikipedia.org/wiki/Elizabeth_Jennings_Graham)

308.

Puppy pregnancy syndrome is a psychosomatic illness in which people believe puppies are growing inside them.

Reference: (https://en.wikipedia.org/wiki/Puppy_pregnancy_syndrome)

309.

The ancient dog breed Xoloitzcuintli, the dog from Coco, was nearly extinct by 1950 and was revived from a group 10 pure bred when an expedition scoured most of Mexico in search for them.

Reference: (https://en.wikipedia.org/wiki/Mexican_Hairless_Dog)

310.

George Washington never had any children because smallpox likely made him sterile.

Reference: (https://en.wikipedia.org/wiki/George_Washington)

311.

Adirondack Park in New York is the largest in the contiguous United States and larger than Yellowstone, Everglades, Glacier, and Grand Canyon National Park combined.

Reference: (https://apa.ny.gov/About_Park/index.html)

312.

Julie Andrews initially turned down the role of Mary Poppins because of her pregnancy. Walt Disney however insisted, saying "we'll wait for you".

Reference: (https://en.wikipedia.org/wiki/Julie_Andrews#Film_stardom)

313.

China and India went to war during the Cuban Missile Crisis.

Reference: (https://en.wikipedia.org/wiki/Sino-Indian_War)

314.

The Kee Bird was a B-29 that crashed in Greenland in 1947 and restored in the 1990s to airworthy condition. However, it burned to the ground when the APU caught fire. No one was seriously injured.

Reference: (http://articles.latimes.com/1995-05-24/news/mn-5487_1_air-force-base)

315.

Bird eggs, like robins, are blue because they are in a balance between warming the egg from absorbed light and protecting the inside from transmitted light and UV.

Reference: (https://www.reddit.com/user/Kalarix)

316.

Irish men sharing the same surname, even very common ones, are approximately 30 times more likely to share a Y-chromosomal haplotype than a random pair of Irish men.

Reference: (https://www.ncbi.nlm.nih.gov/pubmed/16408222?dopt=Abstract)

317.

Gabriel Iglesias was on season 6 of "All That".

Reference: (https://youtu.be/Rd0Hlx_GVWM)

318.

Gladiators never said "Hail emperor, we who are about to die salute you!", that was said only by prisoners about to be killed in the mock naval battles.

Reference: (https://www.ancient.eu/gladiator/)

319.

Vulture bees feed on rotting meat instead of pollen or nectar, while essentially making the equivalent of meat honey.

Reference: (https://en.wikipedia.org/wiki/Vulture_bee)

320.

There are two different bands called UB40. Each is actively touring and has founding members from the original band that was together for nearly 30 years.

Reference: (https://en.wikipedia.org/wiki/UB40)

321.

The United States Coast Guard qualifies as the twelfth largest navy in the world.

Reference: (https://en.wikipedia.org/wiki/United_States_Coast_Guard)

322.

Every champion of the Scripps National Spelling Bee has been Indian-American since 2007, as have 16 of the last 20 winners.

Reference: (https://en.wikipedia.org/wiki/List_of_Scripps_National_Spelling_Bee_champions)

323.

The 1998 Hit "The Way" by Fastball was inspired by an elderly couple who went missing and later were found dead after driving off a cliff.

Reference: (https://www.texasmonthly.com/list/the-secret-history-of-texas-music/the-way-1998/)

324.

"Red Cross Casualty Dogs," also known as "Ambulance" or "Mercy" dogs, took part and were vital in World War I. Known as "Sanitatshunde", or "sanitary hounds", in Germany, these dogs were equipped with their saddlebags of medical supplies and trained to find the wounded and dying on battlefields.

Reference: (https://owlcation.com/humanities/War-Dogs-of-WWI-First-Great-European-War-World-War-One-1914-1918)

325.

Lydia Taft, a distant relative of President William Howard Taft, was the first woman to vote in America in 1756.

Reference: (https://en.wikipedia.org/wiki/Lydia_Taft)

326.

Inattentional deafness is when someone is concentrating on a visual task like reading, playing games, or watching television and are unresponsive to you talking; they aren't ignoring you necessarily, they may not be hearing you at all.

Reference: (http://www.jneurosci.org/content/35/49/16046)

327.

No evidence suggests Dilophosaurus had a cowl like it does in the Jurassic Park movies. It also stood at about 10 feet tall, not 4 feet. The changes were added to help distinguish it from the Velociraptors.

Reference: (https://en.wikipedia.org/wiki/Dilophosaurus)

328.

Those $1 Dollarita Margaritas Applebee's offered as a special promotion were concocted with the cheapest of tequilas and a lot of water.

Reference: (http://awkwardmom.com/applebees-just-gave-something-one-dollar-bills/)

329.

Two young girls from England convinced the world, and the author of Sherlock Holmes, of the existence of fairies through five cleverly manipulated photographs taken from 1917 to 1920. The women only admitted that the Cottingley Fairies were hoax in their 80s, but still claim one picture is real.

Reference: (http://hoaxes.org/photo_database/image/the_cottingley_fairies/)

330.

The "Bueller? Bueller?" scene in "Ferris Bueller's Day Off" was ad-libbed. Actor Ben Stein, also an economics writer and former Nixon advisor, rattled off the lecture about tariffs and supply-side economics off the top of his head.

Reference: (https://spectator.org/62058_love-strange/)

331.

Reinsurance is insurance for insurance companies to help pay large payouts like natural disasters.

Reference: (https://en.wikipedia.org/wiki/Reinsurance)

332.

Canadian dollars have tactile feature, kind of like Braille, that let's visually impaired people recognize money.

Reference: (https://en.wikipedia.org/wiki/Canadian_currency_tactile_feature)

333.

One slice of Costco Cheese pizza has 700 Calories, or 28% of your daily suggested caloric intake.

Reference: (https://www.fatsecret.com/calories-nutrition/costco/cheese-pizza)

334.

To Scientologists the year 1990 is 40 AD, the number of years that have passed since L. Ron Hubbard published "Dianetics" in 1950.

Reference: (http://www.latimes.com/local/la-scientology062890-story.html)

335.

Contrary to popular belief, diplomatic missions such as embassies and consulates are usually not extraterritorial, and people born on U.S. military bases aren't citizens by birth.

Reference:(https://en.wikipedia.org/wiki/List_of_common_misconceptions#Law,_crime,_and_military)

336.

After the Persian Emperor, Khorsow I, captured the city of Antioch in 540, he built a replica city that translates as "Better than Antioch, Khorsow built this". He then moved the inhabitants of Antioch to live in their replica home.

Reference: (https://en.wikipedia.org/wiki/Weh_Antiok_Khosrow)

337.

Vin Diesel wrote, directed and starred in film "Multi-Facial", a film about struggles of multi-racial actors in Hollywood. Spielberg was impressed by the film and especially wrote the role of Adrian Caparzo for Diesel to star in "Saving Private Ryan," giving him his first major role.

Reference: (https://www.popsugar.com/entertainment/Vin-Diesel-Short-Film-Multi-Facial-37225487)

338.
There is one remaining Mister Donut in the U.S.

Reference: (https://thoughtandsight.com/the-last-mister-donut-in-the-us/)

339.
George Lucas, Steven Spielberg and Lawrence Kasdan covered a house in mics for brainstorming "Raiders of the Lost Ark." George Lucas heavily pushed for Indy to have had an affair with Marion Ravenwood when she was only 11 years old.

Reference: (https://www.newyorker.com/culture/culture-desk/spitballing-indy)

340.
The seed of an apricot contains cyanide and if consumed, can result in cyanide poisoning.

Reference: (https://en.wikipedia.org/wiki/Apricot_kernel)

341.
Toots Hibbert was hit in the head by a thrown bottle during a show, costing him months of performances. After the fan was charged, Toots sent a letter to the judge pleading for the fan's release.

Reference: (https://en.wikipedia.org/wiki/Toots_Hibbert)

342.
There's an octopus that changes shape and color to impersonate other fish and snakes to avoid predators.

Reference: (https://www.wired.com/2015/12/absurd-creature-of-the-week-the-octopus-that-does-incredible-impressions-of-fish-and-snakes/)

343.
It actually snows on Mars, however, the snow vaporizes before it can reach the ground.

Reference: (https://en.wikipedia.org/wiki/Climate_of_Mars#Weather)

344.
Helicopters are used in cherry farming to dry cherries after it rains so they don't soak in too much water and explode.

Reference: (http://www.abc.net.au/news/rural/2015-01-14/farmers-assessing-rain-damage-to-fruit-crops/6016918)

345.

An 8-year-old Taiwanese girl had an 8-foot 6-inch tapeworm growing inside of her gut after eating sushi.

Reference: (https://www.independent.co.uk/life-style/health-and-families/tapeworm-sushi-contaminated-eight-foot-long-alive-taiwan-raw-fish-a7791041.html)

346.

Croutons are made out of bread.

Reference: (https://www.allrecipes.com/recipe/6887/croutons/)

347.

16 years after Abraham Lincoln's assassination, Garfield was assassinated at a train station in Long Branch, New Jersey. Robert Lincoln, Abraham's first son, was present for both killings.

Reference: (https://www.biography.com/people/robert-todd-lincoln-20989843)

348.

There is a world record for how far a pigeon rolls on the ground like a bowling ball; it is 662 feet.

Reference: (http://www.thefranklinnewspost.com/news/local/it-s-a-ball-it-s-a-wheel-no-it/article_0e0f4203-2011-5751-93b6-1783277c7917.html)

349.

The actress who played Ellen on "The Adventures of Pete & Pete" became a pediatric surgeon.

Reference: (https://www.youtube.com/watch?v=6c0UawNvep8)

350.

A local farmer and steward of Stonehenge built the first modern long barrow in 2015, reviving the ancient burial practice in England after thousands of years. It was completely booked within two years.

Reference: (https://en.wikipedia.org/wiki/Tumulus#Modern_barrows)

351.

In the name "Kodak Safety Film," the "safety film" meant that it was a low fire risk rather than an extremely flammable nitrate film base.

Reference: (https://en.wikipedia.org/wiki/Film_base)

352.

In his lifetime, Archduke Franz Ferdinand hunted and killed 274,899 animals.

Reference: (https://www.historyanswers.co.uk/kings-queens/franz-ferdinand-killed-almost-everything-on-his-1893-world-tour/)

353.

In South Korea, there is an urban legend that you will die if you sleep in a closed room at night with an electric fan turned on.

Reference: (https://en.wikipedia.org/wiki/Fan_death)

354.

In 1476, the church of Santa Maria Presso San Satiro in Milan didn't have enough space to be built. The problem was solved by Donato Barmante who created an optical illusion using 3 feet of space which gives the church the impression of being much larger than it is.

Reference: (https://en.wikipedia.org/wiki/Santa_Maria_presso_San_Satiro)

355.

Jimmy Carter and George H.W. Bush are in a tight race to be the oldest living former President; both are currently 93 years old.

Reference: (https://en.wikipedia.org/wiki/List_of_presidents_of_the_United_States_by_age)

356.

The video games Fallout: New Vegas and Horizon: Zero Dawn had the same lead writer.

Reference: (https://www.youtube.com/watch?v=h9tLcD1r-6w)

357.

Mr. Bruce Ismay forever regretted fleeing the sinking Titanic. When he was rescued aboard the Carpathia, he was so upset that he didn't let someone else take his lifeboat seat that he did not speak at all for the rest of the voyage on Carpathia.

Reference: (https://en.wikipedia.org/wiki/J._Bruce_Ismay#RMS_Titanic)

358.

Fever is your body's immune response to viruses and bacteria, in an attempt to "cook" them and prevent them from reproducing as quickly.

Reference: (https://www.scientificamerican.com/article/what-causes-a-fever/)

359.

There was a warehouse called Kanada at Auschwitz-Birkenau. To the prisoners, Canada was a country that symbolized wealth. They, therefore, gave the ironic name Kanada, the German spelling of Canada, to the warehouse area as it was full of possessions, clothing and jewelry.

Reference: (https://www.theholocaustexplained.org/the-final-solution/auschwitz-birkenau/kanada-kommando/)

360.

Hiroaki Aoki moved to New York City from Japan where he would work 7 days a week in an ice cream truck he rented in Harlem. Using the $10,000 he saved from the business, he convinced his father to invest in a four-table teppanyaki restaurant which would be named "Benihana" after the red Safflower.

Reference: (https://en.wikipedia.org/wiki/Hiroaki_Aoki#Biography)

361.

Emily Canellos-Simms held the world's largest fine for an overdue library book at $345.14, which was checked out in 1955. The book was "Days and Deeds." The library charged her 2 cents a day. She found the book 47 years later and presented the library with a check for her fine.

Reference: (http://www.guinnessworldrecords.com/world-records/largest-library-book-fine-paid/)

362.

Muhammad Ali talked a suicidal man from jumping off a ledge in Los Angeles, in 1981.

Reference: (https://www.nytimes.com/interactive/2016/12/21/magazine/the-lives-they-lived-muhammad-ali.html)

363.

The strongest wood grown in America is Black Ironwood, it can be found in Florida.

Reference: (https://www.alansfactoryoutlet.com/75-types-of-wood-ranked-by-janka-hardness-and-how-they-are-used)

364.

In order to boost the sales of his book "Leaves of Grass," American writer Walt Whitman wrote anonymous reviews highly praising his work.

Reference: (http://mentalfloss.com/article/77096/when-walt-whitman-reviewed-his-own-book)

365.

Andrew Carnegie and Henry J. Frick helped rebuild Johnstown, Pennsylvania. After the Johnstown Flood, the multi-millionaires donated thousands in relief efforts and funded town projects.

Reference: (https://en.wikipedia.org/wiki/Johnstown_Flood#Court_case_and_recovery)

366.

John Wayne once portrayed the first Khan of the Mongolian Empire, Genghis Khan in the 1956 film "The Conqueror."

Reference: (https://en.wikipedia.org/wiki/The_Conqueror_(1956_film))

367.

Jessie Roberta Cowan, from Kirkintilloch, Scotland, is known as the Mother of Japanese Whisky. She married Masataka Taketsuru, who had come to Scotland to study chemistry and the art of whisky-making, and she followed him back to Japan, where she provided moral and financial support.

Reference: (http://www.bbc.com/news/uk-scotland-scotland-business-30682239)

368.

At the end of the Gulf War, 20 people died in Kuwait due to falling bullets from celebratory gunfire.

Reference: (https://en.wikipedia.org/wiki/Celebratory_gunfire#Falling-bullet_injuries)

369.

Texas has its own pledge of allegiance that students recite every morning after America's pledge of allegiance.

Reference: (https://www.tsl.texas.gov/ref/abouttx/flagpledge.html)

370.

According to the Royal Institute of Chartered Surveyors in the U.K., 70% of world wealth is in land and real estate.

Reference: (http://www.rics.org/uk/about-rics/responsible-business/united-nations-global-compact/un-global-compact-and-rics-join-forces/)

371.

Joel Silver, producer for some of the greatest action franchises of all time, such as Die Hard, Lethal Weapon, and The Matrix, also was one of the three college kids who created Ultimate Frisbee.

Reference: (https://en.wikipedia.org/wiki/Joel_Silver)

372.

On the morning of Evil Knievel's famous crash at Caesars Palace, he lost his last 100 dollars on blackjack and had a shot of Wild Turkey before heading outside with 2 showgirls to attempt the stunt.

Reference: (https://en.wikipedia.org/wiki/Evel_Knievel#Caesars_Palace)

373.

Australian race driver Peter Janson once legally changed his name to "NGK", one of his sponsors, to circumvent a rule that only allowed a driver's name to be carried above the window line of the race car.

Reference: (https://en.wikipedia.org/wiki/Peter_Janson)

374.

"Vampire Deer", also known as Water Deer, develop long canine teeth that can be controlled by facial muscles to be used as a weapon when fighting rival bucks, or drawn back when eating.

Reference: (https://en.wikipedia.org/wiki/Water_deer)

375.

The racehorse Man o' War won 20 races in a row. He lost his last race in 1919 to a horse named Upset.

Reference: (https://en.wikipedia.org/wiki/Upset_(horse))

376.

Some countries ban black-and-white movies from being shown on television. Director Alexander Payne had to create a special color version of his film "Nebraska" in order for it to be aired in countries like Moldova and Sierra Leone.

Reference: (https://www.telegraph.co.uk/culture/film/film-news/11015642/Nebraska-shown-in-colour-against-directors-wishes.html)

377.

Loggerhead sea turtles are chromophobic, which is a fear of color, to specific colors in the yellow spectrum. This allows them to orientate themselves toward the ocean at birth.

Reference: (https://en.wikipedia.org/wiki/Chromophobia?wprov=sfla1)

378.

The Ancient Greeks approached both eating and drinking alcohol with frugality, to highlight the idea of themselves as poor but free people. They also ate dogs.

Reference: (http://www.cooksinfo.com/food-in-ancient-greece)

379.

In 2009, 6% of the population was at risk for scurvy because of poor diet.

Reference: (https://www.inverse.com/article/8208-for-young-men-and-the-poor-scurvy-the-pirate-disease-is-still-a-thing)

380.

The Canada-USA border runs down the middle of Canusa Street. The street separates Beebe Plain, Vermont from Stanstead, Quebec.

Reference: (https://www.youtube.com/watch?v=EocJm3Dry4E&feature=youtu.be)

381.

During World War I, Americans began calling sauerkraut "liberty cabbage" to distance it from its German origin.

Reference: (https://blogs.illinois.edu/view/25/116243)

382.

There are 43 presidential busts that are twenty feet tall, in a field near Jamestown, Virginia, rescued from a presidential museum that went bust.

Reference: (https://www.smithsonianmag.com/travel/what-43-decaying-president-heads-looks-180958129/)

383.

Deer in the Czech Republic don't cross into Germany, following the example of parents who learned to avoid the electrified fence there during the Cold War.

Reference: (http://www.bbc.co.uk/news/world-europe-27129727)

384.

Oranges are sold in bright red net bags because the color of the net deepens the perceived color of the fruits; this is called Munker's illusion.

Reference: (https://www.itp.uni-hannover.de/fileadmin/arbeitsgruppen/zawischa/static_html/strange.html#Munker)

385.

The Walker Affair was an occurrence in the 19th century where a group of Americans invaded the country of Nicaragua in the hopes of creating a new U.S. slave state.

Reference:(https://ipfs.io/ipfs/QmXoypizjW3WknFiJnKLwHCnL72vedxjQkDDP1mXWo6uco/wiki/Walker_affair.html)

386.

Arch Druid Ed Prynn has built a monumental set of standing stones in the front garden of his Cornish bungalow, where he conducts magical ceremonies.

Reference:(http://www.bbc.co.uk/cornwall/content/articles/2005/04/27/christian_druid_feature.shtml)

387.

Paul the Octopus received death threats after successfully predicting Argentina's loss to Germany.

Reference: (https://www.huffingtonpost.com/2010/07/08/psychic-octopus-received_n_639160.html)

388.

Some species of cone snail use insulin in their venom to cause their prey to become paralyzed from hypoglycemic shock.

Reference: (http://www.pnas.org/content/pnas/112/6/1743.full.pdf)

389.

The Chain Moray has blunt teeth adapted for feeding on crustaceans. It can survive approximately half an hour out of water and can strike at prey with its body partly out of the water.

Reference: (https://en.wikipedia.org/wiki/Echidna_catenata)

390.

J.K. Rowling's inspiration for the Deathly Hallows symbol was the Square and Compass Freemasonry symbol, as she had seen it in the film "The Man Who Would Be King."

Reference: (http://www.bbc.co.uk/newsbeat/article/41795562/jk-rowling-reveals-the-inspiration-for-the-deathly-hallows-symbol)

391.

In 2009, a drunk New Zealander lost a poker bet and had his name changed to "Full Metal Havok More Sexy N Intelligent Than Spock And All The Superheroes Combined With Frostnova". He found out that it was accepted 5 years later after receiving a confirmation letter.

Reference: (https://www.theregister.co.uk/2014/03/12/nz_name/)

392.

When a decapitated flatworm regrows its head, it gets all its old memories back too.

Reference: (https://blog.nationalgeographic.org/2013/07/16/decapitated-worms-regrow-heads-keep-old-memories/)

393.

Helping people in poor neighborhoods plant flowers and spruce up empty lots can reduce crime. One experiment in Flint, Michigan, reduced crime by over 50% in the neighborhood.

Reference: (https://www.citylab.com/life/2018/03/want-to-fight-crime-plant-some-flowers-with-your-neighbor/556271/)

394.

According to a review of the medical literature, there were 45 caffeine-related deaths reported between 1959 and 2010.

Reference: (https://www.vox.com/science-and-health/2017/5/17/15649722/caffeine-overdose-health-risks-coffee-energy-drinks)

395.

In Ohio, it is OK to cross a double-yellow line to pass someone, subject to certain conditions.

Reference: (https://www.ohiobar.org/ForPublic/Resources/LawYouCanUse/Pages/The-Law-of-Riding-a-Bicycle-in-Ohio.aspx)

396.

The Westin St. Francis Hotel washes all coins passed through them to keep ladies white gloves clean.

Reference: (https://www.atlasobscura.com/places/westin-st-francis-hotel)

397.

The oldest cave paintings in the world were made by Neanderthals 64,000 years ago.

Reference: (https://www.nature.com/articles/d41586-018-02357-8)

398.

ADE 651, the bomb finding "device" that was sold to airports all over the world, was supposed to find dynamite, cocaine and even specific persons if you loaded a Polaroid into it. The scammers were only stopped after thousands died after it failed to detect explosives in Baghdad.

Reference: (https://gizmodo.com/5455692/ade-651-magic-wand-bomb-detector-is-a-fraud-probably-killed-hundreds)

399.

The longest serving Italian Head of Government is Benito Mussolini; 20 years 267 days continuous, which is almost twice as long as anyone else and with 7 years 38 days being the next longest.

Reference: (https://en.wikipedia.org/wiki/List_of_Prime_Ministers_of_Italy_by_time_in_office)

400.

The cigarette market first boomed after inventor James Bonsack spent 5 years developing a machine that could roll 200 cigarettes per minute in order to win $75,000 in prize money. Manual workers could only roll 4 cigarettes per minute before.

Reference: (https://en.wikipedia.org/wiki/James_Albert_Bonsack)

401.

The stereotypical anchor tattoo indicated a sailor had crossed the Atlantic.

Reference: (https://www.military.com/undertheradar/2016/07/here-are-the-meanings-behind-19-classic-sailor-tattoos)

402.

Alfred Savinelli was the first human to smoke 5-MeO-DMT from the venom of the Sonoran Desert Toad, which happens to be the most potent, naturally occurring psychedelic in the world. He went through hundreds of animals before he hit the jackpot with the toad and he did it all on a "hunch".

Reference: (https://youtu.be/00jbzI4bcUw?t=766)

403.

Nazi researchers looked into methods for warming hypothermic inmates to simulate conditions pilots shot down over the ocean would face; it was discovered that sexual intercourse was more effective than warm colonic irrigation.

Reference: (http://allthatsinteresting.com/nazi-research)

404.

The harpy eagle, one of the largest species of eagle, preys primarily on tree-dwelling mammals like sloths, monkeys, and opossums.

Reference: (http://www.pbs.org/wnet/nature/jungle-eagle-harpy-eagle-fact-sheet/7263/)

405.

The oldest musical composition to have survived in its entirety is a 1st century A.D. Greek tune known as the "Seikilos Epitaph". It was found engraved on an ancient marble column used to mark a woman's gravesite in Turkey as an "everlasting sign of deathless remembrance".

Reference: (https://www.history.com/news/what-is-the-oldest-known-piece-of-music)

406.

Ken Marcus, an artist with an adult fetish and BDSM site and photographer for Penthouse and Playboy magazines, was also an artist-in-resident at the Yosemite National Park Museum.

Reference: (https://en.wikipedia.org/wiki/Ken_Marcus)

407.

The Sand Octopus lacks color changing organs so they shoot jets of water to create quick sand and then blast almost a foot into the ground. Then they secrete a mucus to reinforce the walls of their predator proof bunker and use one arm to create a ventilation "chimney".

Reference: (https://www.earthtouchnews.com/natural-world/animal-behaviour/this-octopus-summons-quicksand-to-build-a-predator-proof-bunker/)

408.

Jean Bell was the first black person to appear on the cover of Playboy Magazine and also one of the first African-American Playmates of the Month as Miss October 1969. Bell posed nude again for Playboy in December 1979 and disappeared from public life.

Reference: (https://en.wikipedia.org/wiki/Jean_Bell)

409.

A computer programmer who was dismissed from his job wrote a computer program that deleted software critical to the company's operations and caused the loss of more than $10 million in sales and contracts.

Reference: (https://www.nytimes.com/1998/02/18/nyregion/man-charged-with-sabotage-of-computers.html)

410.

A mysterious object orbiting Earth, called the Black Knight Satellite is a conspiracy theory that has lasted for almost a decade.

Reference: (https://www.vice.com/en_au/article/evan7n/alien-hunters-spent-the-last-century-looking-for-the-black-knight-satellite)

411.

Mississippi is the only state in which drivers can have an open container.

Reference: (https://www.legalmatch.com/law-library/article/open-container-laws-by-state.html)

412.

Before electronic organizers killed them off, the Filofax was the iconic must-have leather-bound loose leaf organizer for the 1980s business world.

Reference: (http://www.abc.net.au/news/2017-05-07/filofax-design-icon-of-the-1980s-business-world/8485410)

413.

The origins of feudalism in Medieval Europe can be traced back to a disastrous period of the Roman Empire called the Third Century Crisis.

Reference: (https://en.wikipedia.org/wiki/Crisis_of_the_Third_Century)

414.

The Nauruan language is only spoken by 6000 on Nauru and its relationship to the other Micronesian languages is not well understood. Even on the small island, there are slightly different dialects spoken.

Reference: (https://en.wikipedia.org/wiki/Nauruan_language)

415.

The creation of the modern conception of pirates is largely attributed to a book published in 1724, whose true author is unknown. It introduced the notion of pirates with missing legs or eyes, burying treasure, and the Jolly Roger. It also influenced the authors of "Treasure Island" and "Peter Pan."

Reference: (https://en.wikipedia.org/wiki/A_General_History_of_the_Pyrates)

416.

Takotsubo Cardiomyopathy, also known as Broken Heart Syndrome, can cause death by weakening heart muscles and can be caused by sudden stress.

Reference: (https://en.wikipedia.org/wiki/Takotsubo_cardiomyopathy)

417.

Technically, there is no city named Tokyo. Tokyo is a prefecture, something like a state, and not a city. Also, there is no city named Tokyo inside of Tokyo Prefecture.

Reference: (https://www.japan-talk.com/jt/new/why-tokyo-isnt-a-city)

418.

The full coastline of Lake of the Woods in Minnesota and Canada is 25,000 miles long, which is roughly the circumference of Earth.

Reference: (https://www.lakelubbers.com/lake-of-the-woods-190/)

419.

An unannounced low-altitude flight by Air Force One in 2009, meant as a photo-op, caused mass panic instead. People evacuated buildings and ran for their lives, imagining another 9/11-type attack.

Reference: (https://petapixel.com/2017/03/23/2009-air-force-one-photo-op-caused-panic-new-york-city/)

420.

An ant mega-colony exists across 3 continents and is thought to contain billions of ants, all of which recognize each other to be from the same colony. The largest part of the colony is in Europe and is thought to spread 6,000 kilometers, or 3,700 miles, along the Mediterranean coast.

Reference: (http://news.bbc.co.uk/earth/hi/earth_news/newsid_8127000/8127519.stm)

421.

Grape-kun, a Humboldt penguin that lived in a zoo in Japan, grew so attached to a cardboard cutout of an anime girl that he lived with it as his wife till his death.

Reference: (https://en.wikipedia.org/wiki/Grape-kun#Attachment_to_anime_character_cutout)

422.

Yokozuna from WWE was Samoan, not Japanese.

Reference: (https://en.wikipedia.org/wiki/Yokozuna_(wrestler))

423.

In most primary schools in Alice Springs, Australia, students, of all races and nationalities, are taught the indigenous language Arrernte as a compulsory language, often alongside French or Indonesian languages.

Reference: (https://en.wikipedia.org/wiki/Upper_Arrernte_language)

424.

Cocaethyline is a substance produced by the body when cocaine and alcohol are consumed together. Its euphoriant properties are so powerful that it causes feelings of acute well-being almost universally among users, but it's also about 25 times more likely to kill you than cocaine alone.

Reference: (https://en.wikipedia.org/wiki/Cocaethylene#Physiological_effects)

425.

IKEA, a company with $27 billion in annual sales, is actually a nonprofit.

Reference: (https://www.onlinemba.com/blog/video-why-is-ikea-a-non-profit/)

426.

On March 13th, 2007, the New Mexico House of Representatives passed a resolution stating that Pluto will always be considered a planet while in New Mexican skies. The Illinois Senate passed a similar resolution in 2009.

Reference: (https://en.wikipedia.org/wiki/Pluto#cite_note-Holden2007-69)

427.

Rolling Stone member Ronnie Wood was diagnosed with lung cancer in 2013, but refused chemotherapy as he didn't want to lose his hair. He instead had part of his lung removed.

Reference: (https://en.wikipedia.org/wiki/Ronnie_Wood#Personal_life)

428.

While most snakes lay eggs, all do not. Some snakes do give live birth.

Reference: (https://en.wikipedia.org/wiki/Snake#Reproduction)

429.

Georg Gärtner was the last German prisoner of war in the United States. He escaped from prison camp in 1945 and was on the FBI's Most Wanted list for 20 years. He surrendered in 1985.

Reference: (https://en.wikipedia.org/wiki/Georg_G%C3%A4rtner)

430.

New York's Adirondack Mountains and Long Island are surprisingly free of basement-level radioactive radon gas, whereas other portions of the state can have significant radon issues.

Reference: (https://www.wadsworth.org/programs/ehs/nuclear-chem/radon)

431.

There exists a photograph of a baby with his mother, grandmother, great-grandmother, great-great-grandmother, and great-great-great-grandmother.

Reference: (https://io9.gizmodo.com/six-generations-of-the-same-family-in-one-photograph-786240922)

432.

When the Queen Elizabeth Way opened to traffic in 1937, it was the first intercity divided highway in North America and featured the longest stretch of consistent illumination in the world.

Reference: (https://en.wikipedia.org/wiki/Queen_Elizabeth_Way)

433.

Abraham Lincoln was once challenged to a duel by a political adversary. Lincoln accepted. Instead of pistols, Lincoln chose swords. Friends intervened and it ended bloodlessly. Lincoln and his opponent laughed it off as being silly and became lifelong friends.

Reference: (https://www.smithsonianmag.com/history/duel-104161025/)

434.

Persistent Genital Arousal Syndrome and sufferer Dale Decker, the family man who, since slipping a disk in his back, and much to the detriment of his well-being, has been experiencing tens of involuntary orgasms a day.

Reference: (https://nypost.com/2014/09/22/the-living-hell-of-the-man-who-orgasms-100-times-a-day/)

435.

The Onondaga and Oneida Indian Nations declared war on the German Empire during World War I, citing mistreatment of Iroquois stranded in Berlin at the outset of the war as their reasoning.

Reference: (https://michaelleroyoberg.com/teaching-native-american-history/onondaga-1917-a-declaration-of-war-and-other-stories/)

436.

The reusable totes at a supermarket actually have a larger carbon footprint than using the standard plastic bags first for groceries then as a trashcan liner.

Reference:(https://assets.publishing.service.gov.uk/government/uploads/system/uploads/attachment_data/file/291023/scho0711buan-e-e.pdf)

437.

Iceland's CCS, carbon capture and storage, produces limestone when C02 is pumped into basalt formations and mineralizes.

Reference: (https://www.theguardian.com/environment/2016/jun/09/co2-turned-into-stone-in-iceland-in-climate-change-breakthrough)

438.

Manual shift is still the majority in the rest of the world, except in the U.S., where automatic is found in 96% of the vehicles.

Reference: (https://www.thezebra.com/insurance-news/2805/manual-vs-automatic/)

439.

The Griggstown Cow was a supposed ghost that wandered New Jersey. In 2002, an arthritic cow matching its description was found trapped in a ravine it could not get out of, where it was euthanized. It is thought to have escaped a farm nearby and only saw humans when during the foggy days.

Reference: (http://weekinweird.com/2011/08/31/ghost-jumped-moon/)

440.

Childless atheist and author Ninon de L'Enclos left her money to the nine-year-old son of her accountant upon her death. This nine-year-old would later be known as Voltaire.

Reference:(https://en.wikipedia.org/wiki/Ninon_de_l%27Enclos#Life_as_a_courtesan_and_author)

441.

The concept of a grinning "Cheshire Cat" predates Alice in Wonderland.

Reference: (https://en.wikipedia.org/wiki/Cheshire_Cat#Origins)

442.

Peter Benchley, author of the classic novel "Jaws," has come to regret writing his shark thriller. He feels responsible for the mistaken view of sharks as evil creatures. He is now one of the world's most dedicated shark conservation activists.

Reference: (https://en.wikipedia.org/wiki/Peter_Benchley)

443.

Silvio Berlusconi, ex-Prime Minister of Italy, got involved in sex scandals. He was accused of throwing a "bunga bunga" party with several prostitutes. At least one of them was underage. They dressed up as nuns and Brazilian soccer player, Ronaldinho Gaucho.

Reference: (http://nationalpost.com/news/bunga-bunga-nu)

444.

Doctor Amanda Hess, who was in the hospital preparing to give birth, put her own delivery on hold to deliver another woman's baby after hearing that the child was in distress and her doctor had left the hospital for a break. After the on-call doctor came back, Doctor Hess went and had her own baby.

Reference: (https://www.nbcnews.com/news/us-news/kentucky-doctor-delivers-patient-s-baby-right-giving-birth-daughter-n787486)

445.

In the 1970's, the pH of rain samples from parts of New York were at 3.3 due to pollution from the rust belt, the same acidity as grapefruit juice. The default pH of rain is 5.1. This prompted the creation of the term "Acid Rain."

Reference: (https://www.sciencehistory.org/distillations/podcast/whatever-happened-to-acid-rain)

446.

Laser canons, which work just like a laser pointer, are in operation by the U.S. Navy. They can shoot down drones silently and instantly, and precisely aim and burn enemy ship's engine.

Reference: (https://youtu.be/tyUh_xSjvXQ)

447.

An architect secretly hid a scavenger hunt for the family of the $8.5 million apartment he was renovating.

Reference: (https://www.nytimes.com/2008/06/12/garden/12puzzle.html)

448.

Pregnant women are about twice as likely to get bitten by mosquitoes as women who aren't pregnant.

Reference: (http://discovermagazine.com/2016/june/20-things-you-didnt-know-about--bug-bites)

449.

New York Constitution, while prohibiting gambling in general, includes the right to play bingo.

Reference: (https://www.dos.ny.gov/info/constitution.htm)

450.

Douglas Adams came up with the title for "The Hitchhikers Guide to the Galaxy" while lying drunk in a field near Innsbruck with a copy of The Hitch-Hikers Guide to Europe. Looking up at the stars, he thought it would be a good idea for someone to write a hitchhiker's guide to the galaxy as well.

Reference:(https://en.wikipedia.org/wiki/The_Hitchhiker%27s_Guide_to_the_Galaxy#Background)

451.

The Bradford Stadium fire killed 56 people in the matter of minutes. A cigarette dropped under a section of seats lit a trash can that had accumulated over the years.

Reference: (https://youtu.be/iIxN3ypB3rw)

452.

Roosters are often neutered and it makes the meat taste better.

Reference: (https://en.wikipedia.org/wiki/Capon)

453.

There's a dinosaur named after Draco Malfoy: The Dracorex.

Reference: (https://en.wikipedia.org/wiki/Dracorex)

454.

Rodrigo Rosenberg Marzano was a Guatemalan lawyer that planned his own assassination in an attempt to frame the President, and other Guatemalan politicians.

Reference: (https://en.wikipedia.org/wiki/Rodrigo_Rosenberg_Marzano)

455.

Alexander Hamilton believed that Senators and the President should be able to serve for life.

Reference: (http://avalon.law.yale.edu/18th_century/debates_618.asp)

456.

Mark Felt, also known as Deepthroat, once had to investigate if the toilet paper brand "Red Cross" was misleading: "My research, which required days of travel and 100s of interviews, produced 2 definite conclusions: 1. Most people did use toilet tissue. 2. Most people did not appreciate being asked about it."

Reference: (https://en.wikipedia.org/wiki/Mark_Felt)

457.

There are "illegal pitches" in women's softball which, when called by the umpire, can change any strike into a ball, without explanation to the coaches.

Reference: (https://www.livestrong.com/article/307749-softball-facts-rules/)

458.

Some Chinese funerals have strippers to boost attendance.

Reference: (http://www.bbc.com/news/world-asia-china-43137005)

459.

In Malawi, it was a common belief that burying infected people would contaminate the soil. Therefore, lepers would be bound and left inside a hollowed out tree to die.

Reference: (https://www.atlasobscura.com/places/the-leper-tree)

460.

In Georgian London, Elizabeth Stokes was a famous boxer whose exchanges with her opponents are preserved in the press of the time. Over the course of her career, Elizabeth primarily fought in boxing matches, although her skills with a short sword and dagger were well-known.

Reference: (http://fightland.vice.com/blog/elizabeth-wilkinson-stokes-championess-of-american-and-of-europe)

461.

The world's largest earthquake, which struck Chile in May of 1960, was so large that it caused a tsunami that killed 185 people in Japan.

Reference: (https://geology.com/records/largest-earthquake/)

462.

The creator of Famous Amos cookies, Wally Amos, was a talent agent in New York City who was the first to sign Simon and Garfunkel. After inventing his brand of cookies, he started a television show where he teaches children and illiterate adults how to read.

Reference: (https://en.wikipedia.org/wiki/Wally_Amos)

463.

The Iberian ribbed newt, when threatened, will puncture its sides with its own ribs. At the same time, a poison secretes and coats the ribs.

Reference: (http://wikipedia.org/wiki/Iberian_ribbed_newt)

464.

During the Great Flood of 1993, one of only two remaining World War II era Admirable-class Minesweepers broke free from its moorings, dragging two riverboats and a helipad downriver, crashing into a bridge. The minesweeper sank, along with one of the riverboats.

Reference: (https://www.missourinet.com/2013/08/01/wwii-minesweeper-sunk-at-st-louis-20-years-ago-today/)

465.

Crested Black Macaque's are the most affectionate monkeys in the world, due to living in a forest full of food where they all want for nothing. They love to hug, blow kisses, share, and make friends.

Reference: (https://www.youtube.com/watch?v=2IPCymrG9hA)

466.

While preparing a speech to create a permanent soil erosion service, Hugh H. Bennett was notified of a dust storm approaching Washington DC. He pushed back meeting with Congress until it was estimated to arrive. He concluded the meeting with opening up the curtains to a dramatic view of a dust storm.

Reference: (https://weta.org/tv/program/dust-bowl/perfectstorm)

467.

The first psychiatric hospital ward was founded in Baghdad in 705.

Reference: (https://en.wikipedia.org/wiki/History_of_mental_disorders#Mesopotamia)

468.

Hammerhead sharks have never killed a human. There have only been 17 unprovoked shark attacks by hammerheads since records begin in 1580 and all were non-fatal.

Reference: (https://www.floridamuseum.ufl.edu/fish/isaf/contributing-factors/species-implicated-attacks/)

469.

Mobile phones are called cell phones because two Bell Lab engineers in 1947 proposed a network of hexagonal cells resembling biological cells so mobile phones in cars could operate from one spot to another seamlessly. The technology to implement their concept didn't exist at the time, however.

Reference: (https://knowledgestew.com/2016/12/why-are-mobile-phones-called-cell-phones.html)

470.

On the World War II memorial in Washington DC, in an unassuming spot, there is a drawing of "Kilroy Was Here", which was a meme of the time.

Reference: (https://www.atlasobscura.com/places/kilroy-was-here)

471.

Coronary Microvascular Disease is a disease that affects the small vessels of the heart. It is extremely difficult to diagnose. Most doctors don't even recognize it as a real disease, making diagnosis and finding treatment very drawn out and difficult.

Reference:(http://www.heart.org/HEARTORG/Conditions/HeartAttack/DiagnosingaHeartAttack/Coronary-Microvascular-Disease-MVD_UCM_450320_Article.jsp#mainContent)

472.

Harold Shipman, the most prolific known serial killer in the world, was a doctor who was "addicted to killing", murdering an estimated 215 to 260 of his patients.

Reference: (https://www.biography.com/people/harold-shipman-17169712)

473.

During World War II, Adolf Hitler would take powdered cocaine twice a day to aid with throat and sinus problems.

Reference: (https://en.wikipedia.org/wiki/Drug_policy_of_Nazi_Germany)

474.

The remake of "The Omen" was released June 6, 2006.

Reference: (https://en.wikipedia.org/wiki/The_Omen_(2006_film))

475.

The Misericorde was a long narrow dagger used for killing wounded soldiers at the end of a battle. It was considered better than dying in pain from infection or from wounds which were not instantly fatal.

Reference: (https://en.wikipedia.org/wiki/Misericorde_(weapon))

476.

Tobacco smoke enemas were used in the 18th century to treat everything from colds to cholera.

Reference: (https://www.interesly.com/tobacco-smoke-enema-blows/)

477.

Before rubber, people used to use fish bladders and sheep intestines as condoms.

Reference: (https://gizmodo.com/5923695/from-fish-bladders-to-the-reservoir-tip-a-history-of-condom-design)

478.

Many Indian languages have their own film industry. There's Tollywood, Deccanwood, Gollywood, Dhollywood, Bollywood, Jollywood, Sandalwood, Mollywood, Kollywood, another Tollywood, and Coastalwood.

Reference: (https://en.wikipedia.org/wiki/Cinema_of_India)

479.

The Porlock Stone Circle in Western England is similar to Stonehenge. The motive for building these is unknown, although some archaeologists believe it is for supernatural reasons.

Reference: (https://en.wikipedia.org/wiki/Porlock_Stone_Circle)

480.

Planets, including Earth, make bizarre, song-like sounds in outer space. NASA instruments have recorded these "songs" and sent them back to Earth, for all to hear.

Reference: (https://www.nasa.gov/vision/universe/features/halloween_sounds.html)

481.

The U.S. Army tried to weaponize Nerf footballs.

Reference: (https://www.military1.com/military-weapons/article/1789012014-how-the-army-tried-to-weaponize-the-nerf-football/)

482.

Writer James Francis Dwyer was sentenced to 7 years in prison for forgery and uttering. He discovered his passion for writing in prison, and has had some of his work published while he was still in prison.

Reference: (https://en.wikipedia.org/wiki/James_Francis_Dwyer)

483.

There are an estimated 3 trillion mature trees on Earth. 30 times the amount of stars in our galaxy.

Reference: (https://en.wikipedia.org/wiki/Tree)

484.

The religious cult, Heaven's Gate, purchased alien abduction insurance which would cover up to 50 members and would pay out $1 million per person.

Reference:(https://en.wikipedia.org/wiki/Heaven%27s_Gate_(religious_group)#Mass_suicide_and_aftermath)

485.

Due to the terrible rains that struck Bethel, New York the day before, Jimi Hendrix, who was the final artist to perform at Woodstock, didn't perform his set until 8:30 AM Monday morning.

Reference: (https://youtu.be/TKAwPA14Ni4)

486.

Director Robert Rodriquez declined to direct "Deadpool" in order to focus his attention on "Spy Kids 4."

Reference: (https://thefilmstage.com/news/robert-rodriguez-not-directing-%E2%80%98deadpool%E2%80%99-newcomer-considered/)

487.

While working at a railway, Richard Sears' station received a shipment of gold watches but the jeweler refused the shipment. Sears got the watches at a reduced rate and sold them to his coworkers who needed to keep accurate time. The success lead to his first mail-order catalog.

Reference: (https://en.wikipedia.org/wiki/Richard_Warren_Sears#Businessman)

488.

Water-induced wrinkles, such as pruney fingers, are not caused by water being absorbed into the skin and causing swelling, but is likely a nervous system and cardiovascular response to water being present on the skin for prolonged periods.

Reference: (https://en.wikipedia.org/wiki/Wrinkle)

489.

Retta, "Parks and Recreations" Donna Meagle, is the niece of Ellen Johnson Sirleaf, Liberia's first female President and a winner of the Nobel Peace Prize.

Reference: (https://www.hollywoodreporter.com/news/parks-recreation-nobel-peace-prize-245753)

490.

Only 91 of the 3,715 animals in the Berlin Zoo survived World War II. After the Soviet occupation of Berlin, most of these remaining animals were eaten by Red Army soldiers or simply "disappeared".

Reference: (https://en.wikipedia.org/wiki/Berlin_Zoological_Garden#cite_note-13)

491.

A company in Japan developed a smoke alarm specifically designed for those with hearing impairments that uses wasabi odor instead of a loud noise. Tests on sleeping people with normal or no hearing show the device waking all of the subject in just two and a half minutes.

Reference: (https://www.cnet.com/news/wasabi-smoke-alarm-raises-a-stink-in-japan/)

492.

You're supposed to remove those foil seals from your yoghurt to prolong freshness.

Reference: (https://www.telegraph.co.uk/news/2017/09/07/argument-finally-settled-whether-should-completely-remove-foil/)

493.

Similar in function to Amber Alerts, Blue Alerts are designed to speed the apprehension of violent criminals who kill or seriously injure local, state, or federal law enforcement officers.

Reference: (https://www.azdps.gov/safety/alerts/blue)

494.

Stroke victims with partial facial paralysis can lose the ability to voluntarily smile on half their face, but can still fully smile when laughing at a joke.

Reference: (https://www.theatlantic.com/health/archive/2013/01/how-smiles-control-us-all/272588/)

495.

The Indian village of Meghalaya, the wettest place on Earth, has trained branches of rubber trees to create natural bridges over rainy valleys.

Reference: (https://www.theatlantic.com/photo/2014/08/meghalaya-the-wettest-place-on-earth/100797/)

496.

The principle of mirror therapy is used to trick the brain into thinking movement has occurred without pain. You place the affected limb behind a mirror, so the reflection of the opposing limb appears in place of the hidden limb.

Reference: (https://www.physio-pedia.com/Mirror_Therapy)

497.

Poisonous food substances are the reason we find bitter taste unpleasant. Our taste buds evolved associating bitter taste to poison because most of the poisonous wild fruits are bitter and nutritious ones, sweet. The feature which protected us for centuries is now causing major health-risks.

Reference: (https://www.sciencedirect.com/science/article/pii/S0960982213004181)

498.

The Nintendo Power Glove, released in 1987, was a variation of the Sayre Glove, created by Electronic Visualization Laboratory in 1977.

Reference: (https://en.wikipedia.org/wiki/Wired_glove)

499.

The song "Africa" by Toto is actually about a boy trying to write a song on Africa, but since he's never been there, he can only tell what he's seen on TV or remembers in the past. This explains the apparently inaccurate line about Kilimanjaro rising above the Serengeti.

Reference: (https://en.wikipedia.org/wiki/Africa_(Toto_song)#Background)

500.

Poland Spring Water is not bottled in Poland, Europe, but in a place similarly called Poland in Maine.

Reference: (https://www.polandspring.com/)

501.

The term "Third World" originated during the Cold War, and was used to refer to countries that were neither aligned with NATO, the "First World", or the Communist Bloc, the "Second World". Under the original definition, Sweden, Finland and Austria are "third world countries".

Reference: (https://en.wikipedia.org/wiki/Third_World)

502.

An extreme aneuploidic sex chromosomal abnormality, meaning more chromosomes than normal, affects around 1/100,000 males. Instead of XY, affected males have XXXXY chromosomes.

Reference: (https://en.wikipedia.org/wiki/49,XXXXY)

503.

Robert Wadlow became famous as the tallest person in recorded history. Wadlow reached 8 feet 11.1 inches, or 2.72 meters, at his death. He reached the height of adult male, which is 5 feet 10 inches, or 1.78 meters, at 7 years old.

Reference: (https://en.wikipedia.org/wiki/Robert_Wadlow)

504.

Sharks, rays and skates use electricity to hunt and can use it to detect smaller fish breathing in the vicinity.

Reference: (https://www.the-scientist.com/?articles.view/articleNo/48748/title/How-Skates--Sharks-Use-Electricity-to-Sense-Prey/)

505.

The opening three syllables to "The Simpsons" theme tune were sung by the composer, Danny Elfman, and two others. Elfman has stated that the royalties from that alone paid for his health insurance for 25 years, and got him into the Screen Actors Guild for vocal work.

Reference: (http://www.classicfm.com/composers/elfman/news/the-simpsons-tim-burton/)

506.

After reproducing, female swordtail fish can grow a sword and turn into a male.

Reference: (https://www.youtube.com/watch?v=Iiqgo0-O-uI)

507.

Bats are very social creatures, sharing food with close friends and remembering all "scrooges" in their surroundings.

Reference: (http://www.biosphereonline.com/2016/06/01/vampire-bat-social-friends-family/)

508.

Jacob Hauugard, a Danish comedian and actor, ran for parliament as a joke and actually won in 1994. Some of his outrageous campaign promises were: Nutella in field rations, more tailwind on bike paths, and better weather. Nutella in field rations was actually implemented.

Reference: (https://en.wikipedia.org/wiki/Jacob_Haugaard)

509.

Attacking parachutists from an aircraft in distress is a war crime.

Reference: (https://en.wikipedia.org/wiki/Attacks_on_parachutists)

510.

Australia's most famous aircraft designer, Fred David, was an Austrian Jew who previously worked for Heinkel, Mitsubishi, and Aichi.

Reference: (https://en.wikipedia.org/wiki/Fred_David)

511.

A species of toad has mustache fights with other toads for mating rights.

Reference: (https://www.wired.com/2014/02/absurd-creature-week-toad-grows-spiky-mustache-stabs-rivals-ladies/)

512.

Every location on Earth gets around 1 total solar eclipse every 350 years.

Reference: (http://time.com/4829265/total-solar-eclipse-beauty-science/)

513.

Japanese "R" and "L" sounds are a combination of both, which is why when Japanese people say the word light and right they both sound like the same word.

Reference: (https://en.wikipedia.org/wiki/Perception_of_English_/r/_and_/l/_by_Japanese_speakers)

514.

There is an opposite to déjà vu: jamais vu is when you do not recognize things, people or places that you feel you're supposed to know. This is often seen medically as a clinical sign, especially in Alzheimer's or dementia patients, or those that are post-coma.

Reference: (https://www.vocabulary.com/dictionary/jamais%20vu)

515.

Jessica Alba was actually kidnapped after having received telephone threats during the production of "Flipper." She was found unharmed in the trunk of a car.

Reference: (http://www.boomsbeat.com/articles/1152/20140312/50-things-you-didnt-know-about-jessica-alba-kidnapped-from-set-childhood-health-complications.htm)

516.

The hapax is a word which appears only once in a writer's collected works or even only once in that entire language.

Reference: (https://www.atlasobscura.com/articles/hapax-legomenon-hapaxes)

517.

Two Nazi soldiers were rescued from a collapsed underground storehouse in 1951, after it collapsed in 1945.

Reference: (https://en.wikipedia.org/wiki/Babie_Do%C5%82y,_Pomeranian_Voivodeship)

518.

The actor who played Dwight's cousin Mose from "The Office" also co-created "Parks and Recreation".

Reference: (https://en.wikipedia.org/wiki/Michael_Schur)

519.

The first driver for Uber became CEO of the company for a short period of time in the early days of the business.

Reference: (http://www.businessinsider.com/ryan-graves-uber-tweet-career-2017-8)

520.

The band Silversun Pickups is named after a liquor store, Silversun Liquors. The store is located at Silver Lake and Sunset Blvd., and they would call their trips there "Silversun Pickups."

Reference: (http://www.laweekly.com/music/like-their-namesake-liquor-store-silversun-pickups-wont-change-with-the-times-6061296)

521.

It is illegal in New Zealand to act as a medium with the intent to deceive.

Reference: (http://www.legislation.govt.nz/act/public/1981/0113/latest/whole.html#DLM53553)

522.

The Columbia River flood basalts were a series of "rift" eruptions that spewed out 174,000 cubic kilometers of lava covering an area of 164,000 square kilometers.

Reference: (https://en.wikipedia.org/wiki/Columbia_River_Basalt_Group)

523.

Spiders could eat up the entire population of humans in 1 year and still be hungry.

Reference: (https://rd.springer.com/article/10.1007/s00114-017-1440-1)

524.

There are about 290 to 363 Australian Aboriginal languages. The relationships between these languages are not clear at present and at the start of the 21st century, fewer than 150 Aboriginal languages remain in daily use.

Reference: (https://en.wikipedia.org/wiki/Australian_Aboriginal_languages)

525.

NASA's Vehicle Assembly Building at Kennedy Space Center in Florida is the tallest one-story building in the world and is large enough, volume four times of the Empire State Building, that rain clouds have been known to form inside.

Reference: (https://en.wikipedia.org/wiki/Vehicle_Assembly_Building)

526.

"Parks and Recreations" was modeled after the parks and recreation department in El Segundo, specifically the lifeguard staff.

Reference: (https://en.wikipedia.org/wiki/El_Segundo,_California)

527.

The Flower Wars was fought between the Aztec Alliance and its enemies. The wars were fought with a set of conventional rules and the purpose was to capture human sacrifices and combat training.

Reference: (https://en.wikipedia.org/wiki/Flower_war)

528.

GM and other companies monopolized the sale of buses and supplies as part of a deliberate plot to purchase and dismantle streetcar systems in many cities in the United States as an attempt to monopolize surface transportation.

Reference: (https://en.wikipedia.org/wiki/General_Motors_streetcar_conspiracy)

529.

Around 460 million tons of sugar is produced every year.

Reference: (https://en.wikipedia.org/wiki/Sugar_industry)

530.

The name "Tanzania" is a compound of the two states that merged to create the country: Tanganyika and Zanzibar.

Reference: (https://en.wikipedia.org/wiki/Tanzania)

531.

The Indian Government changed the composition of the 5 Rupee Coin after they were smuggled into Bangladesh to make razor blades.

Reference: (https://www.moneylife.in/article/indian-five-rupee-coins-being-turned-into-razors-in-bangladesh/2861.html)

532.

Matt Urban is the most decorated infantry officer in U.S. history. He was wounded twice battling tanks with a bazooka. He returned to his unit on the front after shrapnel ripped his leg. Under intense German fire, he ran across open field to a tank, mounted the turret, climbed in and returned enemy fire.

Reference: (https://wikipedia.org/wiki/Matt_Urban)

533.

In the 1930s, Buryat-Mongolia was one of the sites of Soviet studies aimed to disprove Nazi race theories. Soviet physicians studied the "endurance and fatigue levels" of Russian, Buryat-Mongol, and Russian-Buryat-Mongol workers to prove that all three groups were equally able.

Reference: (https://en.wikipedia.org/wiki/Buryats)

534.

Mammoth Mountain in California is a Super Volcano.

Reference: (https://en.wikipedia.org/wiki/Mammoth_Mountain)

535.

In the second century, people believed that the word "Abracadabra" would protect you against malaria given you engrave it on an amulet and have it with you.

Reference: (https://en.wikipedia.org/wiki/Abracadabra)

536.

All flamingoes are born with grey feathers, and turn pink due to their diet of shrimp and algae.

Reference: (http://www.sciencefocus.com/qa/why-are-flamingos-pink)

537.

Babe Ruth was knocked unconscious when he ran into the wall while chasing a foul ball.

Reference: (http://www.shorpy.com/node/23401)

538.

The first time the name "Jessica" was recorded in print was in Shakespeare's Merchant of Venice. The name ultimately comes from a Biblical character named Iscah, who was only mentioned once in one Bible verse as being the niece of Abraham's.

Reference: (https://en.wikipedia.org/wiki/Jessica_(given_name))

539.

Daniel Day-Lewis's father-in-law is playwright Arthur Miller. Day-Lewis first met his wife, Rebecca Miller, while visiting Arthur Miller during the filming of the adaptation of Miller's play the Crucible.

Reference: (https://en.wikipedia.org/wiki/Daniel_Day-Lewis#Personal_life)

540.

A tearful Courtney Love got the whole crowd to call Kurt Cobain an asshole at his funeral.

Reference: (https://speakola.com/eulogy/for-kurt-cobain-by-courtney-love-1994)

541.

The popular American folk song "Yankee Doodle" was sung by British soldiers to mock the rebelling colonists who they considered to be country rubes. The colonists quickly changed the lyrics and adopted it as their own to insult the British right back.

Reference: (https://www.loc.gov/teachers/lyrical/songs/yankee_doodle.html)

542.

Benjamin Franklin believed that, while marriage is the preferred state for a male, unmarried men should have sex with older women.

Reference: (http://www.swarthmore.edu/SocSci/bdorsey1/41docs/51-fra.html)

543.

A typical lightning strike is about 5 times hotter than the surface of the Sun, measuring at 50,000 degrees Fahrenheit.

Reference: (https://www.weather.gov/safety/lightning-temperature)

544.

The color fuchsia is named after the fuchsia plant, which is named after botanist Leonard Fuchs. This makes it a color named after a plant named after a man named after an animal, as "Fuchs" is German for "fox".

Reference: (https://en.wikipedia.org/wiki/Fuchsia)

545.

Mosquitoes are not attracted by light but by the CO_2 we exhale.

Reference: (https://www.ibtimes.co.uk/mosquitos-smell-carbon-dioxide-human-breath-skin-527830)

546.

The creators of "Parks and Recreation" did research for the show by interviewing actual government officials. One said, "Well, I'm a libertarian, so I don't really believe in the mission of my job. Yes, I'm aware of the irony." The character of Ron Swanson was born.

Reference: (http://latimesblogs.latimes.com/showtracker/2009/11/parks-and-recreation.html)

547.

"Le Rodeur", a French slave ship that set sail with captured Africans in 1819, had such dire conditions onboard that the entire crew and human cargo of 182, bar one, became infected and lost their eyesight at sea. Reports of the tragedy inspired a world renowned anti-slavery poem.

Reference: (http://www.bartleby.com/372/232.html)

548.

Ramen is the new form of currency in prison.

Reference: (https://www.npr.org/sections/thesalt/2016/08/26/491236253/ramen-noodles-are-now-the-prison-currency-of-choice)

549.

MMA was done at the ancient Greek Olympic Games in 648 BC. It was called Pankration and was the only event that wasn't reinstated with the creation of the modern Olympics.

Reference: (https://en.wikipedia.org/wiki/Pankration)

550.

Every New Year's Day in Scotland since 1986, a polar plunge event called Loony Dook has been held. The event was initially jokingly suggested as a hangover cure, but has been repeated every year since then for charity.

Reference: (https://en.wikipedia.org/wiki/Loony_Dook)

551.

A Jesuit living with the Naskapi Innu was horrified when discovering the tribe was not monogamous, so he asked a male how he could be sure the male's son was actually his. He replied, "Thou hast no sense. You French people love only your own children; but we all love all the children of our tribe."

Reference: (http://museum.state.il.us/pub/dmmweb/Jesuit%20Relations/JR06to15.HTM)

552.

10% of ancient tools uncovered are designed for being left-handed, indicating that in the last 10,000 years the proportion of the population that is left-handed has remained consistent at 10%.

Reference: (http://www.rightleftrightwrong.com/history_prehistory.html)

553.

Emma Watson hides books on Subway's in England and New York.

Reference: (http://time.com/4554660/emma-watson-instagram-book-club/)

554.

Enindhilyagwa is an Australian Aboriginal language spoken by the Warnindhilyagwa people. A 2001 Australian government study identified more than 1000 speakers and it was cited in a study on whether humans had an innate ability to count without having words for numbers.

Reference: (https://en.wikipedia.org/wiki/Enindhilyagwa_language)

555.

In 1932, Northern Irish protesters sang "Yes! We Have No Bananas" because not enough people knew the words to any protest songs that weren't specifically Catholics or Protestants.

Reference: (https://en.wikipedia.org/wiki/Yes!_We_Have_No_Bananas)

556.

Aeroflot Flight 593 was an airplane that crashed into a mountain range in Russia, after no technical malfunctions were found. Investigators learned from cockpit voice recordings that the pilot let his 16 year old son use the controls, while thinking that autopilot was on.

Reference: (https://en.wikipedia.org/wiki/Aeroflot_Flight_593)

557.

There has been an uninterrupted human presence in space ever since October 31st, 2000, when the crew of Expedition 1 went to the International Space Station.

Reference: (https://en.wikipedia.org/wiki/Expedition_1)

558.

The practice of consistently describing Democratic states as blue and GOP ones as red came about in the aftermath of the 2000 election when networks needed a quick way to refer to who won a state; prior to this party coloration was left up to the networks, which often showed the Democrats as red.

Reference: (https://en.wikipedia.org/wiki/Red_states_and_blue_states)

559.

In three years, a pair of rats can have half a billion descendants.

Reference: (https://www.qsrmagazine.com/news/how-quickly-rats-can-breed-terrifying)

560.

Millennial males were significantly more likely than millennial females to live with mom and dad. One theory is that sons may have an easier time at home since parents expect their sons to do less housework than their daughters.

Reference: (https://www.marketwatch.com/story/more-men-than-women-live-with-their-parents-2013-08-02)

561.

The legal reason champagne is only produced in Champagne, France, is due to the Treaty of Versailles, which reaffirmed that rule among the nations that signed it.

Reference: (https://en.wikipedia.org/wiki/Champagne#Right_to_the_name_Champagne)

562.

Shahid Azmi who was falsely imprisoned for 7 years. He spent most of his sentence at the library studying law and working to prove his innocence. He then became a lawyer to help free other people who have been falsely convicted.

Reference: (https://en.wikipedia.org/wiki/Shahid_Azmi)

563.

Benazir Bhutto, Pakistan's first female Prime Minister, had an arranged marriage when she was 34 while campaigning for the role.

Reference: (https://www.nytimes.com/1987/07/31/world/benazir-bhutto-to-marry-in-a-pact-by-2-families.html)

564.

Oxygen masks in airplanes aren't connected to an oxygen tank. Instead, they use a chemical reaction to generate it on the spot.

Reference: (https://en.wikipedia.org/wiki/Chemical_oxygen_generator)

565.

In the 1969 EC-121 shootdown incident, North Korean jets shot down a reconnaissance plane in international airspace killing 30 Americans. America never retaliated.

Reference: (https://en.wikipedia.org/wiki/1969_EC-121_shootdown_incident)

566.

Michael Jackson recorded "Behind the Mask" for Thriller but managerial disputes prevented its release until after his death. The song was a hit and has been described as, "a fiercely funky cousin to Wanna Be Startin' Somethin'".

Reference: (https://en.wikipedia.org/wiki/Behind_the_Mask_(Michael_Jackson_song))

567.

From May 1918 to Feb 1921, the Menshevik dominated Democratic Republic of Georgia existed.

Reference: (https://www.europenowjournal.org/2017/12/28/the-legacy-of-the-georgian-revolution/)

568.

When actor and cowboy Slim Pickens joined the military during World War II, he stated his profession was "rodeo", the recruiter heard "radio" and Slim spent the entire war as a radio operator.

Reference: (https://en.wikipedia.org/wiki/Slim_Pickens)

569.

The Mapuche, indigenous inhabitants of Chile and southern Argentina, resisted the Spaniard conquest during the long "Arauco War" with their resistance lasting more than 350 years. They were the only indigenous people who were never conquered by the Spanish.

Reference: (https://en.wikipedia.org/wiki/Arauco_War)

570.

Taschen published a limited edition set of "Hugh Hefner's Playboy" featuring never-seen-before artwork, correspondence and 700 pages of personal text. Every set is autographed by Hefner and comes with a piece of the Playboy's legendary silk pajamas.

Reference: (https://www.freshnessmag.com/2009/12/14/hugh-hefners-playboy-6-volumes-an-illustrated-biography/)

571.

The City of Vernon, California, only has 112 residents. The city government owns almost all homes in its borders, and city officials have made more than $1 million governing the city.

Reference: (https://en.wikipedia.org/wiki/Vernon%2C_California)

572.

In 2013, Pimsleur Language Programs donated 15 lessons of its Tagalog course to support aid agencies and volunteers in the wake of Typhoon Haiyan.

Reference: (https://www.prnewswire.com/news-releases/pimsleur-language-programs-offers-free-tagalog-language-course-to-aid-typhoon-haiyan-yolanda-relief-and-recovery-efforts-233310261.html)

573.

Gene Simmons will deliver a 10-CD box set and spend 2 hours at your house for a fee of $50,000.

Reference: (https://www.inc.com/jeff-haden/yes-for-50000-gene-simmons-of-kiss-will-actually-come-to-your-house.html)

574.

Manchester may have been named after a breast-shaped hill.

Reference: (https://en.wikipedia.org/wiki/Manchester#Name)

575.

In 2005, two women had a competition in Europe's largest brothel to see who could have more partners in a day. They would pay any man 50 euros to have sex with them. Over the course of 11 hours, they had sex with 115 men, and they had to turn away another 1700 men.

Reference: (https://en.wikipedia.org/wiki/Pascha_(brothel))

576.

Neil Armstrong took a recording of Dvořák's "New World Symphony" to the Moon during the Apollo 11 mission in 1969.

Reference: (https://en.wikipedia.org/wiki/Anton%C3%ADn_Dvo%C5%99%C3%A1k)

577.

The Ancient Egyptians believed that the God Atum created the universe by masturbating to ejaculation.

Reference: (https://en.wikipedia.org/wiki/Masturbation#Compulsive_masturbation)

578.

The horned lizard has the ability to squirt blood out of its eyes if it feels threatened by other animals. They do this by restricting blood flow from the head, which cause blood cells to rupture in their eyes.

Reference: (https://en.wikipedia.org/wiki/Horned_lizard)

579.

The word "ambulance" is written backwards on the front of the vehicle because drivers in front will be able to read it easily in their rear view mirror.

Reference: (https://en.wikipedia.org/wiki/Mirror_writing)

580.

Fantasy author Peter V. Brett wrote most of his first novel, "The Painted Man", on his phone during his commute.

Reference: (http://www.petervbrett.com/2007/11/15/subway-writing/)

581.

Some Hopis tried to stop the publication of a Hopi Dictionary by the University of Arizona because they were upset that other people might learn their language. The publisher responded it could not restrict the book to Hopis only, but only scholars would be expected to buy the dictionary.

Reference:(https://en.wikipedia.org/wiki/Hopi_Dictionary:_Hop%C3%ACikwa_Lav%C3%A0yt utuveni)

582.

"Human" is a surname. The U.S. census data shows a ranking number of 17725 in 1990 and 15845 in 2000 for Human surnames on the Popularity Index.

Reference: (http://www.pbs.org/pov/apps/thesweetestsound/popularity-index/popindex.php?name=Human&Submit=Submit)

583.

SpongeBob SquarePants creator Stephen Hillenburg majored in marine sciences at Humboldt State University and minored in art. He loved both subjects but his real passion was art, he chose marine science because he thought it would be hard to make a living doing art alone.

Reference: (https://en.wikipedia.org/wiki/Stephen_Hillenburg#Early_life_and_education)

584.

Every baby is colorblind when it is born.

Reference: (http://discoveryeye.org/rods-and-cones-they-give-us-color-and-night-vision/)

585.

George Ulrich, an American geologist, fell into lava and survived.

Reference: (https://en.wikipedia.org/wiki/George_Ulrich_(American_geologist))

586.

From March 1945 to December 1947, Romania was a "Communist Monarchy" under Soviet influence.

Reference: (https://en.wikipedia.org/wiki/Michael_I_of_Romania#Reign_under_communism)

587.

Keikaimalu is the world's first known surviving wholphin, which is a hybrid between a male killer whale and a female bottlenose dolphin.

Reference: (http://allthatsinteresting.com/wholphin)

588.

From 1790 to 1800, Philadelphia was the State Capital as well as the Capital of the United States; this forced both the state and national legislatures to meet in same the building.

Reference: (http://cpc.state.pa.us/history/the-history-of-pennsylvanias-early-capitols.cfm)

589.

During the 1998 East Java Ninja Scare, the deaths of religious leaders were ascribed to mysterious sorcerer-assassins wearing black, resulting in mass hysteria.

Reference: (https://en.wikipedia.org/wiki/1998_East_Java_ninja_scare)

590.

Vatican City has its own football league.

Reference: (https://en.wikipedia.org/wiki/Vatican_City_Championship)

591.

Cannabis is part of the cannabaceae, which is part of the Urticales order. The word Urticales comes from the Latin word "urtica" which means skin rash. That is why cannabis fan leaves give you an itchy rash.

Reference: (https://en.wikipedia.org/wiki/Urticales)

592.

Non-citizens could vote in many U.S. states well into the 20th century. 1928 was the first national election in which no non-citizens could vote legally anywhere.

Reference: (https://en.wikipedia.org/wiki/Right_of_foreigners_to_vote_in_the_United_States)

593.

The "car recall formula" bit from "Fight Club" was based on an actual situation where there was a known defective gas tank with the Ford Pinto.

Reference: (http://www.tortdeform.com/archives/2006/10/the_formula_1.html)

594.

The city of Cleveland was originally spelled "Cleaveland". However, when a local newspaper couldn't fit the whole name into the header, they dropped the first "A" and the spelling stuck.

Reference:(https://en.wikipedia.org/wiki/History_of_Cleveland#Survey_and_Founding_of_the_City:_1796%E2%80%931860)

595.

The city of Industry, California, has over 80,000 people working there, but is home to only 219 residents.

Reference: (https://en.wikipedia.org/wiki/City_of_Industry,_California)

596.

In the 2001 and 2002 season, basketball legend Michael Jordan donated his entire salary to 9/11 relief efforts.

Reference: (https://www.nba.com/wizards/news/WSEedfund_011016.html)

597.

A 12 ounce drip coffee has more caffeine than two shots of espresso.

Reference: (https://www.kickinghorsecoffee.com/en/blog/caffeine-myths-espresso-vs-drip)

598.

In the year 2000, China placed a ban on console gaming. It wasn't until just nearly three years ago that the restrictions were lifted.

Reference: (http://money.cnn.com/2015/07/27/technology/china-video-game-ban-lifted/)

599.

Cats can't taste sweet things.

Reference: (http://www.catster.com/lifestyle/cat-health-are-pineapple-leaves-poisonous-toxic-cats)

600.

Melanesia Sergeant Major Jacob Vouza was captured by the Japanese, hung from a tree and beaten with rifles, tied to a red ant hill, bayonetted seven times in the chest and once in the throat, but still managed to chew through his restraints and deliver news of the impending attack.

Reference: (https://en.wikipedia.org/wiki/Jacob_C._Vouza)

601.

"The Brave Little Toaster" very nearly took home the top award at the 1988 Sundance Film Festival, but the judges were afraid that the festival would lose respect by picking a cartoon.

Reference: (https://en.wikipedia.org/wiki/The_Brave_Little_Toaster#Release_and_home_media)

602.

Prior to MetroCards replacing tokens on New York City subways, some booth attendants would sprinkle chili powder in coin slots to stop people from "coin sucking".

Reference: (http://gothamist.com/2015/01/23/subway_token_suckers.php)

603.

You are 10 times more likely to get bitten by a New Yorker than a shark.

Reference: (https://www.floridamuseum.ufl.edu/shark-attacks/odds/compare-risk/nyc-biting-injuries/)

604.

In 1993, a 16 year old Brooklyn teen pretended to be a subway conductor and drove a train for 3 hours before being caught.

Reference: (https://www.nytimes.com/1993/05/12/us/subway-caper-fueled-by-passion-for-trains.html)

605.

Until 2008, 12 AM was "noon" and 12 PM was "midnight" according to the United States Government Printing Office.

Reference: (https://en.wikipedia.org/wiki/12-hour_clock#Confusion_at_noon_and_midnight)

606.

Some lakes can literally explode, causing a mini-tsunami and a deadly cloud of gas that is capable of killing thousands miles away.

Reference: (https://en.wikipedia.org/wiki/Limnic_eruption)

607.

Some of the famous red pigments of Pompeii were originally yellow, until the heat of Vesuvius changed them.

Reference: (https://www.theguardian.com/science/2011/sep/22/pompeii-red-yellow)

608.

Wang Chung isn't actually a guy named "Wang Chung," but a group, and the name is Chinese, meaning "Yellow Bell," and is the first musical note in the Chinese classical music scale.

Reference: (https://en.wikipedia.org/wiki/Wang_Chung_(band))

609.

Colombia has the highest amount of banks per capita, with 256.8 branches per 100,000 people. The U.S. for comparison has 32.7 branches and Switzerland, which is renowned for its banking, has 42.5. The world average is 12.5.

Reference:(https://data.worldbank.org/indicator/FB.CBK.BRCH.P5?end=2016&start=2016&view=chart&year_high_desc=true)

610.

North and South Korea had a second Korean War known has the Korean DMZ Conflict between 1966 and 1969.

Reference: (https://en.wikipedia.org/wiki/Korean_DMZ_Conflict)

611.

Female anglerfish can grow to sizes of 3.3 feet, or 1 meter, in length and 100 pounds, or 45 kilograms, in weight. The source of their luminescence comes from a symbiotic bacteria that live inside their enclosed cup-shaped reflector organ called the esca.

Reference: (https://en.wikipedia.org/wiki/Anglerfish)

612.

If you were to stand at the top of the Olympus Mons on Mars, the tallest planetary mountain in the Solar System, you would not be able to tell you were on a mountain due to the shallow slope in the mountain extending further than the horizon line, which is a mere three kilometers away.

Reference: (https://www.space.com/20133-olympus-mons-giant-mountain-of-mars.html)

613.

Lincoln Logs were created by John Lloyd Wright, son of Frank Lloyd Wright.

Reference: (https://www.incredibleart.org/links/jlwright/lloyd_wright5.html)

614.

The most expensive Big Mac in the world is in Switzerland, where a Big Mac cost $6.35 apiece.

Reference: (https://amp.businessinsider.com/most-expensive-big-mac-in-the-world-switzerland-2017-1)

615.

The 1975 film "Breakout" was successful partially because of Columbia Pictures' use of the then-new strategy of "saturation booking", and its success paved the way for Universal's promotion of "Jaws".

Reference: (https://en.wikipedia.org/wiki/Breakout_(1975_film)#Reception)

616.

The Japanese national anthem was composed by a German.

Reference: (https://en.wikipedia.org/wiki/Franz_Eckert)

617.

Former president of Brazil, Fernando Collar, practiced black magic and animal sacrifices while in office.

Reference: (https://www.nytimes.com/1993/04/14/world/rio-de-janeiro-journal-the-collor-story-cont-much-ado-about-magic.html)

618.

Caffeine can cause a sense of panic attacks, especially on those prone to anxiety.

Reference: (http://straightfromthedoc.com/caffeine-and-anxiety/)

619.

Supernovas are thought to vibrate and emit an audible hum right before exploding.

Reference: (https://www.space.com/2054-stellar-sound-waves-set-supernovas.html)

620.

Blueberries and raspberries have the same pigment compounds, anthocyanins. Blueberries are blue because they are less acidic. If you add an acid like vinegar to crushed blueberries, they will turn red. Adding a base like baking soda will return them to blue.

Reference: (https://en.wikipedia.org/wiki/Anthocyanin#In_food)

621.

There are now more mattress stores in the U.S. than Starbucks.

Reference: (https://www.sleepzoo.com/now-mattress-stores-us-starbucks/)

622.

A "Touch Cube" is a Rubik's Cube for blind people, where the colors also have different little embossed shapes on them.

Reference: (https://eu.rubiks.com/store/puzzles/rubiks-touch-cube/)

623.

Trijicon, a firearm optics company, secretly hid Bible verse references in serial numbers of scopes mass purchased by the U.S. Armed Forces, such as "ACOG4X32JN8:12" referencing John 8:12—"I am the light of the world." This controversy spawned the nickname "Jesus rifles".

Reference: (https://en.wikipedia.org/wiki/Trijicon_biblical_verses_controversy)

624.

The original sound of the lightsaber was created in "Star Wars." It was developed by sound designer Ben Burtt as a combination of the hum of idling interlock motors in aged movie projectors and interference caused by a television set on a shield-less microphone.

Reference: (http://filmsound.org/starwars/burtt-interview.htm)

625.

In the 1970s, researchers at Xerox PARC invented personal computers with graphical user interfaces, and other modern features. The project was brushed aside by Xerox, and nearly a decade later, one man was invited by Xerox PARC to see the inventions. That man was Steve Jobs.

Reference: (http://www.pbs.org/nerds/part3.html)

626.

Russia tried to establish a colony in Africa in 1889, in Sagallo, which is modern day Djibouti.

Reference: (https://en.wikipedia.org/wiki/Sagallo)

627.

Michigan has the second longest coastline in the U.S., next to Alaska.

Reference: (https://www.michigan.gov/som/0,4669,7-192-26847-103397--,00.html)

628.

Prince Charles is one of Britain's most successful living painters.

Reference: (https://www.vanityfair.com/style/2016/02/prince-charles-painting-watercolors)

629.

Lion fish are a big concern around Florida and the Bahamas. Derbies and Tournaments are set up with food vendors to hunt and eat the invasive but tasty fish.

Reference: (https://www.smithsonianmag.com/science-nature/lionfish-invaded-army-divers-chefs-fighting-back-180968999/)

630.

In the 1962 World Cup, the Chilean team ate Swiss cheese before beating Switzerland, spaghetti before beating Italy, and drank vodka before beating the USSR. Then they drank coffee before their match against Brazil but lost.

Reference:(https://en.wikipedia.org/wiki/History_of_the_Chile_national_football_team#1962_World_Cup)

631.

Maggots have many utilities. Certain species feed on dead tissue and also eat bacteria, making them useful for wound debridement. In forensic science, the presence and development of maggots on a corpse can also be used to approximate the time of death.

Reference: (https://en.wikipedia.org/wiki/Maggot#Medical_treatment)

632.

The late great musician Prince was a fantastic bowler who could throw a strike at will and wore knee high furry boots while he was doing it.

Reference: (http://themalestrom.com/picturing-prince-steve-parke-exhibition/)

633.

The John Denver song "Take Me Home, Country Roads" actually has little lyrical association with West Virginia. Some believe it may actually refer to western Virginia.

Reference: (http://wikipedia.org/wiki/Take_Me_Home,_Country_Roads)

634.

The Designated Hitter rule in Major League Baseball was suggested by Philadelphia Athletics manager Connie Mack in 1906, although Mack wasn't the first to suggest it, but it gained little support.

Reference: (https://en.wikipedia.org/wiki/Designated_hitter#Background_and_history)

635.

The General Slocum disaster was the New York area's worst disaster in terms of loss of life until the September 11, 2001 attacks. It is the worst maritime disaster in the city's history, and the second worst maritime disaster on United States waterways.

Reference: (https://en.wikipedia.org/wiki/PS_General_Slocum)

636.

The serial killer Harvey Glatman was presenting himself as a photographer for pulp fiction magazines to find his victims and take photos of them tied before they even knew that they were kidnapped.

Reference: (https://en.wikipedia.org/wiki/Harvey_Glatman)

637.

Nearly 90 percent of patients who had "penicillin allergy" listed on their medical charts were found to actually have no such allergy at all.

Reference: (https://www.thedailybeast.com/so-you-might-actually-not-be-allergic-to-penicillin)

638.

The comedian George Carlin was the voice of Mr. Conductor and the Narrator for Thomas the Tank Engine.

Reference: (https://en.wikipedia.org/wiki/George_Carlin#Television)

639.

In South Korea, only visually impaired people can be licensed masseurs; dating back over 100 years to a Japanese colonial rule set up to guarantee the blind a livelihood.

Reference: (https://uk.reuters.com/article/oukoe-uk-korea-blind/south-korea-court-says-only-blind-can-be-masseurs-idUKTRE49T1RG20081030)

640.

According to a congressional report, there are an estimated 2.4 million cases of unnecessary surgery sold and performed on the public every year. Lucian Leape, a former surgeon and professor at the Harvard School of Public Health, a renowned patient safety expert cautions people who are advised to get surgery by physicians.

Reference: (https://www.usatoday.com/story/news/nation/2013/06/18/unnecessary-surgery-usa-today-investigation/2435009/)

641.

A Japanese startup received a whopping $90 million funding just to put up a billboard on the Moon by 2020, and thus kick-start the lunar economy.

Reference: (https://www.biztechpost.com/japanese-startup-plans-colonizing-moon/)

642.

In the late 1960s and early 1970s, award-winning author and screenwriter Larry McMurtry felt so unappreciated that he started wearing a t-shirt that read "Minor Regional Novelist".

Reference: (https://legacy.lib.utexas.edu/taro/tsusm/00048/tsu-00048.html)

643.

In addition to a common language family, religions from a wide swath of Eurasia, from Iceland to Italy to India, share numerous mythemes. This suggests a common cultural origin.

Reference: (https://en.wikipedia.org/wiki/Proto-Indo-European_religion)

644.

There are invisible tornados. Tornados get their color from debris, but over an open field they can be "invisible".

Reference: (https://youtu.be/vjNTDcjSYMU)

645.

The Pokémon Ditto was based off the original copy machines called Dittos which copied print in a purple ink.

Reference: (http://www.retroland.com/dittos/)

646.

Pop group Spandau Ballet are named after a World War I phenomenon where corpses hit by gunfire would appear to dance.

Reference: (https://en.wikipedia.org/wiki/Spandau_Ballet)

647.

The younger brother of Paul Angelis, the man who voiced Ringo Starr in the movie, "Yellow Submarine," replaced Ringo Starr as the Narrator for Thomas the Tank Engine.

Reference: (https://en.wikipedia.org/wiki/Michael_Angelis)

648.

Marie Antoinette's famous quote, "Why don't they eat cake", is actually attributed to a Chinese Emperor saying: "Why don't they eat meat?"

Reference: (http://www.cjdelling.com/pen/drawing-let-them-eat-cake/)

649.

Bruno, in 2004, was the first bear seen in Germany after 170 years. He was ordered to be hunted down as it was worried his preference for chickens and beehives would led to him attacking humans.

Reference: (https://en.wikipedia.org/wiki/Bear_JJ1)

650.

A Mormon missionary in the 1850s declared himself to be the second coming of Christ and started a new religious movement. His movement ended when he attempted to "ascend into Heaven" by jumping off of a cliff in front of all his followers.

Reference: (https://en.wikipedia.org/wiki/Arnold_Potter)

651.

In 1993, a 5 year old set his house on fire, killing his 2 year old sister. The mother blamed Beavis and Butt-head for making fire seem "cool." As a result, MTV removed all references of fire from their past and future episodes and rescheduled it for 10:30 PM instead of 7:00 PM.

Reference: (http://articles.baltimoresun.com/1993-10-24/news/1993297147_1_beavis-and-butt-head-tv-and-film-shows)

652.

Grover Cleveland is the only president to have a wedding in the White House.

Reference: (https://www.history.com/news/125-years-ago-nice-day-for-a-white-house-wedding)

653.

Tania Head was a fake 9/11 attack survivor. She was supposedly on the 78th floor and lost her husband. This was all revealed a fraud when a reporter investigated. It turns out she wasn't even in the U.S. on September 11.

Reference: (https://www.aol.com/amp/2016/09/10/tania-head-fake-survivor-september-11/)

654.

Voltaire wrote more than 2,000 books during his life.

Reference: (https://www.onthisday.com/articles/voltaire-writer-wit-philosopher-and-rebel)

655.

Tilda Swinton was considered for the role of Pennywise in the 2017 version of "It."

Reference: (https://en.wikipedia.org/wiki/It_(2017_film))

656.

The Yugoslav frigate Split is the only ship in the world which shelled the city it is named after.

Reference: (https://en.wikipedia.org/wiki/Yugoslav_frigate_Split)

657.

Nestle Smarties are all the same flavor except the orange one, which is flavored with orange oil.

Reference: (http://www.nestle.co.uk/brands/chocolate_and_confectionery/chocolate/smarties)

658.

30% of Canada speaks French, and French is the official language of Quebec.

Reference: (https://en.wikipedia.org/wiki/Languages_of_Canada)

659.

Valentina Tereshkova became the first woman in space on June 16, 1963, where she spent three days orbiting the Earth 48 times, and is the only woman to have completed a solo space mission.

Reference: (https://en.wikipedia.org/wiki/Valentina_Tereshkova?repost)

660.

During the Battle of Koh Tang, 85 Cambodian soldiers fiercely defended the island against 3 U.S. marine battalions inflicting 88 casualties.

Reference: (https://www.warhistoryonline.com/vietnam-war/mayaguez-incident-the-last-battle-of-the-vietnam-war-b.html?full-theme=1)

661.

In reality, condoms are only 85% effective against pregnancy.

Reference: (https://www.plannedparenthood.org/learn/birth-control/condom/how-effective-are-condoms)

662.

Michael Keaton started his acting career on Mister Roger's "Neighborhood." His first role was as the Black and White Panda, listed under the name Michael Douglas.

Reference: (http://www.neighborhoodarchive.com/mrn/episodes/1435/index.html)

663.

There are no evidence of any lost continent and the idea of a lost continent has been completely rejected by theory of plate tectonics.

Reference: (https://en.wikipedia.org/wiki/Mu_(lost_continent)#Geological_arguments)

664.

20% of all children born in The Netherlands in 2013 were born at home and not in a hospital.

Reference: (http://www.bbc.com/news/health-22888411)

665.

Volkswagen sold more sausages than cars in 2015.

Reference: (https://www.independent.co.uk/news/business/news/vw-volkswagen-currywurst-sausages-emissions-scandal-a6883751.html)

666.

More than half of the internet traffic is coming from bots.

Reference: (https://voluum.com/blog/traffic-coming-bots-eating-ad-budget/)

667.

Neil Armstrong also went to the North Pole, sixteen years after walking on the Moon.

Reference: (https://en.wikipedia.org/wiki/Neil_Armstrong#North_Pole_expedition?)

668.

90% of East Asians are lactose intolerant. In contrast, only 5% of Northern Europeans are lactose intolerant.

Reference: (https://ghr.nlm.nih.gov/condition/lactose-intolerance)

669.

To understand a pun, the brain's left and right hemispheres have to work together due to the unique structure of the joke.

Reference: (https://www.scientificamerican.com/article/your-pun-divided-attention-how-the-brain-processes-wordplay/)

670.

In Norway, from the 1950s to the 1980s, corpses had to be wrapped in plastic before being placed in a coffin and buried. It was later discovered that the bodied didn't decompose properly. A lime injection process was developed to allow the bodies to decompose and the graves to be reused.

Reference: (https://www.gizmodo.com.au/2013/10/norway-is-overrun-with-plastic-covered-corpses-that-refuse-to-rot/)

671.

North Brother Island is a completely desolate and abandoned island right in the middle of New York City that no one is allowed to visit.

Reference: (http://uk.businessinsider.com/north-brother-island-photo-tour-2017-9?utm_source=facebook&utm_medium=cpc&utm_campaign=auddev-test4000115/)

672.

Saint Elizabeth Ann Seton is the Patron Saint of seafarers, Catholic schools, Shreveport, Louisiana, and the State of Maryland.

Reference: (https://en.wikipedia.org/wiki/Elizabeth_Ann_Seton)

673.

There are gnotobiotic, or germ free, animals.

Reference: (https://youtu.be/Gv8H2F5cBG8)

674.

Nitroglycerin is used to widen blood vessels for easier blood flow and to increase the pumping power of the heart, as a treat or prevention of chest pain.

Reference: (https://www.webmd.com/heart-disease/nitroglycerin-chest-pain#1)

675.

Cars were equipped with phones as early as 1946.

Reference: (https://en.wikipedia.org/wiki/Car_phone)

676.

Only 1.1% of Jamaicans practice Rastafarianism.

Reference: (https://www.cia.gov/library/publications/the-world-factbook/geos/jm.html)

677.

The World's Spiciest Ice Cream is so hot, you need to sign a death waver first.

Reference: (https://nerdist.com/spiciest-ice-cream-death-waiver/)

678.

Ancient Sumerians are responsible for the world's oldest fart joke. Dating back to 1900BC, the Sumerian joke reads: "Something which has never occurred since time immemorial; a young woman did not fart in her husband's lap."

Reference: (http://news.bbc.co.uk/2/hi/7536918.stm?2)

679.

Norwegian commando Jan Baalsrud's patrol was ambushed by the Germans and he was the only survivor. He evaded capture for two months, suffering severe snow blindness and frostbite, and was forced to amputate his own toes to prevent gangrene before being whisked to safety in Sweden.

Reference: (https://en.wikipedia.org/wiki/Jan_Baalsrud#World_War_II)

680.

The famous Swedish Ice Hotel is now required to include fire alarms, despite being made entirely out of frozen water.

Reference: (http://newsfeed.time.com/2013/11/15/swedish-ice-hotel-required-to-install-fire-alarms/)

681.

When 5 experts were given fingerprints that, unbeknownst to them, they had deemed a "match" earlier in their career, and told that these were from a suspect of the Madrid train bombings, 4 of the 5 experts now said that they didn't match, suggesting their judgement is affected by the context.

Reference: (https://www.huffingtonpost.com/jeff-kukucka/forensic-evidence_b_3178848.html?guccounter=1)

682.

In 2012, the Museum of Modern Art accepted 14 video games as part of its permanent collection.

Reference:(https://en.wikipedia.org/wiki/List_of_video_games_in_the_Museum_of_Modern_Art#Wishlist)

683.

Microsoft rescued Apple from the brink of bankruptcy back in 1997 with a $150 million investment.

Reference: (https://www.industryleadersmagazine.com/greatest-business-lessons-from-the-rivalry-between-steve-jobs-and-bill-gates/)

684.

Michael Jackson's "Thriller" was originally called "Starlight" and it featured different lyrics.

Reference:(https://www.youtube.com/watch?v=0_Eb7MYSPd4&index=3&list=RDobvf95aCyWs)

685.

The "Call of the Void" is the feeling when you think about jumping off a high place but don't actually want to do it.

Reference: (http://allthatsinteresting.com/call-of-the-void)

686.

Eddie Murphy has 9 kids with 5 different women.

Reference: (https://en.wikipedia.org/wiki/Eddie_Murphy#Family)

687.

The Correlates of War project defines war as a conflict in which there are 1,000 battlefield deaths. This means the Falklands War, with 907 deaths, does not qualify as a war, while the 100-hour-long "Soccer War" between El Salvador and Honduras, with about 2,000 fatalities, does.

Reference: (https://www.nytimes.com/2011/06/29/opinion/29iht-edgvosdev29.html)

688.

Octopuses have three hearts and their blood is blue in color. The blue-ringed octopus is one of the most venomous animals known; the venom of one could kill ten grown men.

Reference: (http://www.softschools.com/facts/animals/octopus_facts/23/)

689.

There's a type of amputation where the leg is rotated and the foot is used as a joint for the knee.

Reference: (https://www.amputee-coalition.org/resources/an-explanation-of-rotationplasty/)

690.

The building on the cover of Led Zeppelin's "Physical Graffiti" album is a New York City tenement block located at 96 and 98 St. Mark's Place New York City, New York in the East Village.

Reference: (http://www.feelnumb.com/2009/07/27/led-zeppelin-physical-graffiti-cover-location/)

691.

When Steven Spielberg re-enrolled at California State 16 years ago, they gave him 3 points credit in paleontology for his work on "Jurassic Park."

Reference: (https://speakola.com/grad/steven-spielberg-harvard-university-2016)

692.

Alan Turing was a fantastic marathon runner, running just shy of the 1948 Olympic standards.

Reference: (https://en.wikipedia.org/wiki/List_of_non-professional_marathon_runners)

693.

Tribes on the Andaman Islands have evolved in isolation for so long that their languages are mutually unintelligible from their closest neighbors, and particular genes are unlike any other population on the planet.

Reference:(http://digitalcommons.wayne.edu/humbiol/vol85/iss1/5?utm_source=digitalcommons.wayne.edu%2Fhumbiol%2Fvol85%2Fiss1%2F5&utm_medium=PDF&utm_campaign=PDFCoverPages)

694.

The Foo Fighters' 1997 sophomore album "The Color and the Shape" is named after a bowling pin the tour manager bought at a thrift store in which he described it as the reason he bought it.

Reference:(https://en.wikipedia.org/wiki/The_Colour_and_the_Shape#Recording_and_production)

695.

The U.S. army spent roughly $18 billion on the Future Combat Systems and delivered 0 production vehicles.

Reference: (https://www.defensenews.com/30th-annivesary/2016/10/25/30-years-future-combat-systems-acquisition-gone-wrong/)

696.

Semantic satiation is a psychological phenomenon in which repetition causes a word or phrase to temporarily lose meaning for the listener, who then perceives the speech as repeated meaningless sounds.

Reference: (https://en.wikipedia.org/wiki/Semantic_satiation)

697.

"Abracadabra" is based loosely on the Hebrew Phrase "I will create as I speak", and the Aramaic phrase "I create like the word."

Reference: (http://aramaicnt.org/2014/01/29/abracadabra-is-not-aramaic/)

698.

The Copper Hill Cheese-Rolling and Wake is a competition where competitors chase after a piece of cheese rolling down a hill.

Reference: (https://en.wikipedia.org/wiki/Cooper%27s_Hill_Cheese-Rolling_and_Wake)

699.

The Starbucks logo was originally a bare breasted eagle spread mermaid screaming "Buy Coffee!"

Reference: (http://www.cnn.com/2010/LIVING/04/09/starbucks.trivia/index.html)

700.

Rock band Van Halen included, "a bowl of M&M candies, with absolutely all the brown ones removed", as an indicator whether the concert promoter had actually read the band's complicated contract. It served as a quick check to ensure safety of all equipment.

Reference: (http://www.thisisinsider.com/van-halen-brown-m-ms-contract-2016-9)

701.

The ages of the Disney Princesses are: Jasmine from Aladdin 15, Pocahontas 18, Cinderella 19, Mulan 16, Tiana from The Princess and the Frog 19, Ariel from The Little Mermaid 16, Rapunzel from Tangled 18, Belle from Beauty and the Beast 17, Aurora from Sleeping Beauty 16, and Snow White is 14.

Reference: (http://disney.wikia.com/wiki/Disney_Princess?2)

702.

In November 2013, the bodies of the Jamison family were found in a wooded area in southeast Oklahoma. Their pick-up truck was discovered less than three miles away containing phones, $32,000 in cash as well as the family dog. No cause of death was determined.

Reference: (http://www.the13thfloor.tv/2016/05/04/the-disturbing-unexplained-mystery-of-the-jamison-family-disappearance/)

703.

Giant African rats, known unofficially as HeroRats, or officially as Mine Detection Rats are used in Africa and Cambodia to detect land mines. They are more effective than humans or dogs at finding dynamite.

Reference: (http://www.bbc.com/future/story/20130222-scratch-and-sniff-mine-detectors)

704.

During the filming for "The Order of the Phoenix," Alan Rickman banned Rupert Grint and Matthew Lewis from coming within 5 meters of his new BMW, because during the making of the "Goblet of Fire," they spilled milkshakes in his other car.

Reference: (http://www.thisisinsider.com/15-behind-the-scenes-secrets-from-the-harry-potter-movies-2018-1#alan-rickman-didnt-let-the-cast-come-near-his-bmw-11)

705.

The slung term for the main rotor retaining nut in a helicopter is "Jesus nut". The term was coined by American soldiers in Vietnam because if the pin in the "Jesus nut" were to fail the only thing the crew could do is to "pray to Jesus."

Reference: (https://en.wikipedia.org/wiki/Jesus_nut)

706.

Stanford Medical categorizes sleep deprivation as an epidemic among teens with 87% of high school students getting less than the recommended amount of sleep.

Reference: (https://med.stanford.edu/news/all-news/2015/10/among-teens-sleep-deprivation-an-epidemic.html)

707.

Iron Butterfly bassist Philip Taylor Kramer committed suicide in 1995, but his body wasn't found until four years later.

Reference: (https://en.wikipedia.org/wiki/Philip_Taylor_Kramer)

708.

Prince's label had to send floppy discs with a special font on it to the media after changing his name to a symbol, so they could type it.

Reference: (https://tonedeaf.com.au/remembering-prince-changed-name-symbol-sent-font-discs/)

709.

There was an ideology created by John Lennon which involves wearing a bag over your entire body to promote peace and equality in the 1960s.

Reference: (https://en.wikipedia.org/wiki/Bagism)

710.

The Korean DMZ Conflict, otherwise known as the Second Korean War, was a series of border clashes between North and South Korean forces on the DMZ which resulted in hundreds dead.

Reference: (https://en.wikipedia.org/wiki/Korean_DMZ_Conflict)

711.

There's a London skyscraper that melted cars and set buildings on fire in 2013.

Reference: (https://www.nbcnews.com/science/how-london-skyscraper-can-melt-cars-set-buildings-fire-8c11069092)

712.

The first instance of airmail was back in 1859 via balloon.

Reference: (https://www.wired.com/2010/08/0817us-airmail-balloon/)

713.

There exists such a thing as "anti-paparazzi" clothing, coated in glass nanospheres which reflect light from camera flashes and results in images taken of the wearer coming back horrendously overexposed.

Reference: (https://petapixel.com/2015/02/25/watch-flashback-anti-paparazzi-clothing-ruin-flash-photographs/)

714.

There is a phobia of erect penises called Phallophobia.

Reference: (https://en.wikipedia.org/wiki/Phallophobia)

715.

Judy Melinek was a medical examiner who identified hundreds of bodies from the 9/11 World Trade Center attacks, many of which were merely scraps of flesh or pieces of limb. She was called in mid-August 2002 because they had found a foot bone on top of another skyscraper 1/5 mile away.

Reference: (http://www.nydailynews.com/news/national/doctor-details-grim-work-identifying-9-11-bodies-new-book-article-1.1873374)

716.

The silver maple tree in Toronto that inspired the Canadian patriotic song "The Maple Leaf Forever" fell in 2013, but some of the wood was made into two guitars that are passed on to different musicians.

Reference: (http://www.cbc.ca/news/canada/windsor/toronto-s-maple-leaf-forever-tree-on-tour-with-blue-rodeo-tragically-hip-1.3078035)

717.

Slime mold is an amoeba that group together forming a multicellular structure to find food with staggering intelligence for a no-brain organism. Slime molds haveen been known to solve math problems, find the most efficient way to food, remember it and even anticipate periodic, regulated changes.

Reference: (https://www.youtube.com/watch?v=mOI-JlNcDVs&feature=youtu.be)

718.

Charles Ingram cheated his way up to a million dollars in the world famous "Who Wants to be a Millionaire" TV show.

Reference: (https://www.youtube.com/watch?v=HIGtLRnGCD4&feature=youtu.be)

719.

Peter III of Russia placed a rat on trial under martial law for chewing one of his toy soldiers. The rat was found guilty and was hung by the neck in a makeshift set of mini gallows.

Reference: (https://didyouknowfacts.com/time-russian-tsar-rat-court-martialed-executed/amp/)

720.

Walt Disney created EPCOT as a response to the "dirty" cities of America. It was planned to be a business community focused on developing new ideas for urban living. After his death in 1966, the plan was abandoned and a theme park based off of the idea was built instead.

Reference: (https://en.wikipedia.org/wiki/EPCOT_(concept))

721.

The philosophical poems of Pope John Paul II were turned into a vocal jazz album titled "The Planet Is Alive...Let it Live!" and despite being performed by four-time Grammy award winner Sarah Vaughan, the album was described as "difficult to sit through" and "a bit pompous."

Reference: (https://en.wikipedia.org/wiki/The_Planet_Is_Alive...Let_it_Live!)

722.

The "Diderot Effect" is where, if a person buys something that is deviant from their usual style, it can often trigger a wave of uncharacteristically risky purchases, in an impulsive effort to switch to the new style.

Reference: (https://en.wikipedia.org/wiki/Diderot_effect)

723.

The world "purple" has only one perfect rhyme: "curple". Curple refers to the narrowest part of the waist before the hips flare out; alternatively, the bum.

Reference: (https://en.wikipedia.org/wiki/Purple#18th_and_19th_centuries)

724.

The process of transforming sound to shape is called Cymatics.

Reference: (https://www.tokenrock.com/explain-cymatics-16.html)

725.

Richard Gatling, the inventor of what is considered to be the first machine gun, had actually hoped that the tremendous power of his new weapon would discourage large scale battles and show the folly of war; eventually leading to significantly lower death tolls in future conflicts.

Reference: (https://www.history.com/topics/gatling-gun)

726.

Bannerstones were extraordinary, symmetrical artifacts created by prehistoric Native Americans that still mystify scientists. They may have started as atlatl counterbalances but later evolved into ceremonial objects.

Reference: (https://www.archaeology.org/issues/262-1707/features/5626-native-american-bannerstones)

727.

Carlsberg Special Brew was created in honor of Winston Churchill after his role in World War II.

Reference: (https://www.telegraph.co.uk/news/shopping-and-consumer-news/11339977/Five-things-you-never-knew-about-Special-Brew.html)

728.

90% of the coal we burn today comes from dead trees of the Carboniferous period.

Reference: (http://phenomena.nationalgeographic.com/2016/01/07/the-fantastically-strange-origin-of-most-coal-on-earth/)

729.

Roselle was a guide dog who led her blind master out of the World Trade Center to survival on 9/11.

Reference: (https://www.akc.org/expert-advice/news/feature/meet-the-9-11-dogs-roselle-who-helped-her-blind-partner-escape-the-wtc/)

730.

The American government made a movie clip in the midst of the Cold War about a turtle who should "duck and cover" in the hopes of teaching young children about surviving a nuclear war.

Reference: (https://www.youtube.com/watch?v=IKqXu-5jw60&feature=youtu.be)

731.

A Viennese baker copied the shape of crescent on Turkish flag to create a celebratory dish of victory in 1683, known as croissant.

Reference: (https://frenchmoments.eu/the-formidable-story-behind-the-french-croissant/)

732.

In 1859, there was an Aurora so powerful that it powered telegraph networks across America and Europe, in some cases causing damage and sparks from the amount of power it generated.

Reference: (https://en.wikipedia.org/wiki/Aurora#Auroral_events_of_historical_significance)

733.

A face with big eyes, a small nose, and a small chin exhibits Kinderschema: the collection of traits humans have evolved to find adorable.

Reference: (https://www.powerofpositivity.com/science-explains-makes-people-think-something-cute/)

734.

Nearly a quarter of American Presidents have been Episcopalian, despite only 2% of the population observing that faith.

Reference:(https://en.wikipedia.org/wiki/Religious_affiliations_of_Presidents_of_the_United_St ates#List_of_Presidents_with_details_on_their_religious_affiliation)

735.

The green flash is an optical phenomenon that occurs during sunset or sunrise. The color green is occasionally visible for a few seconds, and it happens because the Earth's atmosphere can separate the light into the spectrum.

Reference: (http://earthsky.org/todays-image/photo-double-green-flash-san-diego)

736.

There was a black samurai who served under the daimyō Oda Nobunaga who praised him for his strength and was given his own residence and a short, ceremonial katana by Nobunaga. When they first met, Nobunaga suspected his skin was covered in ink and had his skin scrubbed.

Reference: (https://en.wikipedia.org/wiki/Yasuke)

737.

During World War I, soldiers were so fearful of chemical attacks that some imagined that they had been poisoned even though they hadn't.

Reference: (https://www.ncbi.nlm.nih.gov/pmc/articles/PMC2376985/)

738.

Jackie Robinson's brother named Mack was an athlete and a great runner. He won a Silver Medal in the 200 meters behind Jesse Owens during the 1936 Summer Olympics in Berlin, Germany.

Reference: (https://www.nytimes.com/2000/03/14/sports/mack-robinson-85-second-to-owens-in-berlin.html)

739.

J.K Rowling is still the only writer to become a billionaire. However, she lost her billionaire status from giving away much of her earnings to charity.

Reference: (https://en.wikipedia.org/wiki/J._K._Rowling)

740.

Donnie Yen, the blind monk in "Star Wars: Rogue One," was once leaving a Hong Kong nightclub with his girlfriend when they were attacked by a gang who had been bothering them earlier in the night. Donnie hospitalized 8 of them.

Reference: (https://en.wikipedia.org/wiki/Donnie_Yen#Real_fighting_experience_and_prowess)

741.

Clowns paint their faces onto eggs to copyright them so other clowns can't use the same face. There is a registry of egg faces in both Europe and in the United States.

Reference: (https://www.atlasobscura.com/articles/why-smart-clowns-immortalize-their-makeup-designs-on-ceramic-eggs)

742.

Shaggy's real name is Norville Rogers.

Reference: (https://en.wikipedia.org/wiki/Shaggy_Rogers)

743.

Tool's popular song "46&2" is based on the ideas of Carl Jung that state the possibility of reaching a state of evolution at which the body would have two more than the normal 46 chromosomes.

Reference: (https://en.wikipedia.org/wiki/Forty_Six_%26_2)

744.

Project Isabela is a "conservation" effort to remove invasive species from the Galapagos Islands. Tens of thousands of goats and pigs were killed.

Reference: (https://www.galapagos.org/conservation/our-work/ecosystem-restoration/project-isabela/)

745.

Like canaries in a coal mine, cats served as an early-warning indicator of mercury poisoning when they displayed signs of having developed "Dancing Cat Fever", in which the cats would convulse and leap to the sea.

Reference:(http://content.time.com/time/specials/packages/article/0,28804,1986457_1986501_1986450,00.html)

746.

The College of the Ozarks doesn't charge tuition. Instead, students work on campus at least 15 hours a week and have two 40-hour work weeks.

Reference: (https://owlcation.com/academia/Free-Tuition-Colleges)

747.

It's forbidden to die on Svalbard because bodies don't decompose because of the cold.

Reference: (http://news.bbc.co.uk/2/hi/programmes/from_our_own_correspondent/7501691.stm)

748.

The smallest of the eight main Hawaiian Islands, Kahoolawe and its surrounding waters are by law off-limits to the public. The only way ashore is through volunteer work opportunities offered throughout the year.

Reference:(https://www.hawaiimagazine.com/blogs/hawaii_today/2009/12/18/how_to_visit_Kah oolawe)

749.

The Jackson 5's original audition tape sent to Motown Records in August 1967 was rejected. They were turned down again after a second taped audition in July 1968. They were finally signed in 1969 and went on to have four number one singles within a year and became Motown's best-selling group.

Reference: (https://en.wikipedia.org/wiki/The_Jackson_5#Early_years)

750.

Built in 1923 by James Dole, who developed the pineapple industry in Hawaii, Hotel Lanai was the first and only hotel on the Hawaiian Island until 1990.

Reference: (https://www.bizjournals.com/pacific/news/2014/07/31/billionaire-larry-ellison-buys-historic-hotel.html)

751.

At the time of the European arrival at Haida Gwaii in 1774, it is estimated that Haida speakers numbered about 15,000. Smallpox, venereal disease and tuberculosis reduced the population and it currently has about 20 native speakers.

Reference: (https://en.wikipedia.org/wiki/Haida_language)

752.

Record label executives that granted Stanley Kubrick permission to use "Also Sprach Zarathustra" in "2001: A Space Odyssey" thought the movie would cheapen the song so they didn't allow the conductor or orchestra to be named. After the film came out they rushed to capitalize on it.

Reference:(https://en.wikipedia.org/wiki/2001:_A_Space_Odyssey_(soundtrack)#Album_release)

753.

In 2003, a single track and field athlete won the team state title in South Dakota.

Reference: (https://www.yankton.net/sports/article_af918d3c-5d76-11e8-9404-1b7942df31db.html)

754.

A Japanese "artist" cooked and served his own genitals in a banquet in Tokyo.

Reference: (https://www.huffingtonpost.com.mx/entry/asexual-mao-sugiyama-cooks-serves-own-genitals_n_1543307)

755.

There is a house in Ottawa that was home to two Canadian Prime Ministers and hosted many foreign dignitaries like Roosevelt and Churchill. It was briefly considered for permanent official residence of the Prime Minister.

Reference: (https://en.wikipedia.org/wiki/Laurier_House)

756.

There was a sitcom in the 1990's called "Homeboys in Outer Space" where two astronauts flew around the universe in a winged car, nicknamed "Space Hoopty", in the 23rd century. The duo's car, which was a cross between a lowrider and an 18 wheeler, was piloted by a talking female computer named Loquatia.

Reference: (https://en.wikipedia.org/wiki/Homeboys_in_Outer_Space#Plot)

757.

Between 1968 and 1972, more than 130 American airplanes were hijacked, sometimes more than one on the same day.

Reference: (https://www.vox.com/2016/3/29/11326472/hijacking-airplanes-egyptair)

758.

In the last 20 years, only 3 number one overall picks in the NBA draft have won a championship, Andrew Bogut, Kyrie Irving, and LeBron James, all as members of either the Cleveland Cavaliers or Golden State Warriors.

Reference: (https://en.wikipedia.org/wiki/List_of_first_overall_NBA_draft_picks)

759.

Marin County, California has one of the highest income per capita in the United States and is home to San Quentin Prison as well as George Lucas' Skywalker Ranch.

Reference: (https://en.wikipedia.org/wiki/Marin_County,_California)

760.

There is only one surviving member of the Bee Gees: Barry. Maurice passed in 2003, and Robin in 2012. Their little brother Andy Gibb, who embraced a solo career and sung the 1978 hit Shadow Dancing, died in 1988 at age 30.

Reference: (https://en.wikipedia.org/wiki/Bee_Gees)

761.

The first modern novel about a time machine was not the H.G. Wells one, but "The Anacronópete", which was written by the Spanish author Enrique Gaspar y Rimbau and published 8 years earlier.

Reference: (http://www.bbc.com/news/world-europe-12900390)

762.

Inwood Hill Park contains the largest remaining forest land on Manhattan. Unlike other Manhattan parks, Inwood Hill Park is largely natural, being non-landscaped and has glacial potholes.

Reference: (https://en.wikipedia.org/wiki/Inwood_Hill_Park)

763.

Galactic Tick Day is a day to celebrate the Solar System's progress around the center of our Milky Way Galaxy. The next Galactic Tick Day will fall on June 26, 2018.

Reference: (https://en.wikipedia.org/wiki/Galactic_Tick_Day)

764.

On Apollo 15, a hammer and a feather were dropped on the surface of the Moon to illustrate how objects of different weight fall at an equal rate without air resistance.

Reference: (https://www.cnet.com/news/what-happens-when-you-drop-a-feather-and-a-hammer-on-the-moon/)

765.

The restaurant chain "Rollercoaster Restaurant" makes the food you order get delivered on a small rollercoaster, which includes a loop.

Reference: (https://en.wikipedia.org/wiki/Rollercoaster_Restaurant)

766.

The Pawukon calendar is probably the most complicated one in existence, which has 10 different concurrent weeks with 1 to 10 days each. It is not connected to seasons, or the solar calendar. It doesn't count years, so the calendar has no epoch.

Reference: (https://en.wikipedia.org/wiki/Pawukon_calendar)

767.

The days after Memorial Day are known as the "100 Deadliest Days" for teen drivers, where fatal accidents involving teen drivers increase by 15% compared to the rest of the year.

Reference: (https://www.educateddriver.org/memorial-day-kicks-off-100-deadliest-days-for-teens/)

768.

In 1993, 16-year-old Keron Thomas posed as a train conductor and drove an A train for three hours and safely delivered passengers to their destinations before he accidentally triggered an emergency brake on a fast curve.

Reference: (http://www.nydailynews.com/new-york/man-posed-train-operator-reflects-teen-thrill-article-1.1335852)

769.

The Tesla logo is the cross section of an electric motor.

Reference: (https://electrek.co/2017/01/24/tesla-logo-cross-section-electric-motor/)

770.

Nanjing is officially the safest city in China. However, many older Nanjingese may have a resentment towards the Japanese because of the events during World War II and it is recommended for Japanese tourists to not appear too conspicuously Japanese and keep any opinions to oneself.

Reference: (https://wikitravel.org/en/Nanjing)

771.

A fruit fly only a few millimeters in size produces sperm cells that are almost six centimeters long.

Reference: (http://www.media.uzh.ch/en/Press-Releases/2016/drosophila-giant-sperm.html)

772.

Pangolins are believed to be the world's most trafficked mammal, accounting for as much as 20% of all illegal wildlife trade. Their scales can cost more than $3,000 per kilogram on the black market.

Reference: (https://en.wikipedia.org/wiki/Pangolin_trade)

773.

Rocket exhaust has about the same pressure as the air around it when it exits the nozzle. If it were significantly higher pressure than ambient, more energy will be wasted as the exhaust expands and pushes in all directions, rather than just the direction of flow.

Reference: (https://en.wikipedia.org/wiki/Rocket_engine_nozzle#Atmospheric_use)

774.

The author of "Hoot" also wrote "Strip Tease," the basis for the 1996 Demi Moore movie.

Reference: (https://en.wikipedia.org/wiki/Carl_Hiaasen)

775.

Hugh Hefner described his ideal Playmate in 1967: "She is never sophisticated, a girl you cannot really have. She is a young, healthy, simple girl - the girl next door."

Reference: (https://www.avclub.com/r-i-p-hugh-hefner-1818869256)

776.

In 1999, George Harrison was stabbed repeatedly by an intruder trying to kill him.

Reference: (https://www.nytimes.com/1999/12/31/world/george-harrison-stabbed-in-chest-by-an-intruder.html)

777.

Over 15,000 new chemicals are added to the CAS Registry every day; so far they're at 200 million total.

Reference: (https://en.wikipedia.org/wiki/CAS_Registry_Number)

778.

Candy Land was involved in one of the first disputes over internet domain names in 1996. An adult web content provider registered candyland.com, and Hasbro objected. Hasbro obtained an injunction against the use.

Reference: (https://en.wikipedia.org/wiki/Candy_Land#History)

779.

The first version of a graphing calculator on the original Apple PowerPC computer was made in an Apple office by someone who wasn't formally on Apple's payroll and had to sneak in to code or test the code.

Reference: (http://newsweek.com/they-hacked-real-good-free-117023)

780.

Afghan "cameleers" in 1800 helped Australia shape its outback. These cameleers opened the outback, helped with the construction of the Overland Telegraph Line and Railways, supplied stations with its goods and services, with little recognition.

Reference: (http://www.australiangeographic.com.au/topics/history-culture/2011/07/australias-afghan-cameleers)

781.

The U.S. National Anthem has 4 verses, yet we only typically sing 1 at events.

Reference: (https://amhistory.si.edu/starspangledbanner/the-lyrics.aspx)

782.

In 1998, the city of Topeka, Kansas was renamed ToPikachu, for one day to celebrate Pokémon's debut in the United States.

Reference: (http://www.cnn.com/2010/TECH/03/02/google.kansas.topeka/index.html)

783.

Quotations from Chairman Mao Tse-tung were published in 117 countries and territories around the world by 1967. Some sources claim that over 6.5 billion printed volumes have been distributed. It was an essentially unofficial requirement for every Chinese citizen to own, read, and carry it at all times.

Reference: (https://en.wikipedia.org/wiki/Quotations_from_Chairman_Mao_Tse-tung)

784.

Jean-Claude Van Damme originally played The Predator in the 1987 Arnold Schwarzenegger film, but he hated the role and was subsequently fired.

Reference: (https://www.theverge.com/2014/4/10/5600446/predator-original-alien-costume-jean-claude-van-damme)

785.

Snoop Dogg was the driver in a drive-by-shooting where his bodyguard shot Phillip Woldermarian. Both were acquitted for self-defense.

Reference: (https://en.wikipedia.org/wiki/Snoop_Dogg#Personal_life)

786.

There are over 250 books in the African Writers Series started by Chinua Achebe in 1962. After a fairly successful beginning, the series faced difficulties that mirrored those that faced the continent. By the mid-1980s, only one or two new books were published per year.

Reference:(https://en.wikipedia.org/wiki/African_Writers_Series#List_of_authors_and_books_in_the_African_Writers_Series)

787.

Thomas Edison waged a negative press campaign on Nikola Tesla in order to sell his DC system and undermine Tesla, which failed as Westinghouse Corporation, which had bought patents for Tesla's AC system was chosen to supply the lighting after demonstrations of his AC system by Tesla.

Reference: (https://www.biography.com/people/nikola-tesla-9504443)

788.

In 1995, the Canadian Mounties caused angry protests when they exclusively licensed the marketing of their image to Disney.

Reference: (https://www.mountieshop.com/faqs/)

789.

Naked mole rats can survive with basically no oxygen and their incisors can be moved independently of each other.

Reference: (https://www.youtube.com/watch?v=2sKADUBfdMk)

790.

The iLoo was a cancelled Microsoft project from 2003 to develop a portable toilet where you could browse the Internet. It was so widely ridiculed that Microsoft initially tried, and failed, to pass it off as a hoax.

Reference: (https://en.wikipedia.org/wiki/ILoo?text#Public_relations_timeline)

791.

Australian businessman Dick Smith released "Dickheads" Matches, a pun on the iconic ex-Aussie brand of matches "Redheads", to protest foreign takeover of Aussie brands.

Reference: (https://en.wikipedia.org/wiki/Dickheads_(brand))

792.

The TV Show "Oz" was filmed in the old headquarters of the National Biscuit Company in Manhattan.

Reference: (https://www.nytimes.com/1999/07/12/arts/prison-series-seeks-to-shatter-expectations.html)

793.

Bette Graham became a typist to support herself and her son Michael in 1951. She was a poor typist and invented a white tempera paint to cover her mistakes. This led to her business Liquid Paper Co. which she sold 25 years later for $48 million. Michael went on to become a member of The Monkees.

Reference: (http://www.feelnumb.com/2010/03/04/liquid-paper-and-the-monkees/)

794.

In 1997, at age 17, actress Michelle Williams won the World Cup of Futures Trading Award; no one has surpassed her record since she set it.

Reference: (http://www.worldcupchampionships.com/live-stats-3)

795.

In the United States, a private person can make an arrest, including through use of force, for felonies, misdemeanors, and breaches of peace.

Reference: (https://en.wikipedia.org/wiki/Citizen%27s_arrest#United_States)

796.

Rob Willis bought a used BMW M3 from a dealer and immediately began having issues with the car. While watching an old episode of "Top Gear" he noticed he had been sold the car Jeremy Clarkson had been honing on the show.

Reference: (https://www.carthrottle.com/post/this-guy-bought-a-problematic-bmw-m3-then-saw-his-car-had-been-abused-by-top-gear/)

797.

The Euthyphro Dilemma is found in Plato's dialogue Euthyphro. In the dialogue, Socrates asks Euthyphro the question: "Is what is morally good commanded by God because it is morally good, or is it morally good because it is commanded by God?"

Reference: (https://en.wikipedia.org/wiki/Euthyphro_dilemma)

798.

Cartographers protect their intellectual property by slipping fake streets, or even entire towns, into their maps. If the street or town shows up on another map, they know it was stolen. Dictionary writers have been known to do the same thing with fake words.

Reference: (https://www.atlasobscura.com/articles/trap-streets-with-no-names/)

799.

The captain and crew of the USS Grenadier, after 18 hours of tracking a contact in icy Northern Atlantic waters, forced the surfacing of a Russian Zulu-class missile-firing submarine, providing first proof of the presence of Soviet submarines in the Atlantic during the Cold War.

Reference: (http://www.navy.mil/submit/display.asp?story_id=45746)

800.

The longest-running U.S. daily radio program, King Biscuit Time, is done in small town Helena, Arkansas.

Reference: (https://en.wikipedia.org/wiki/King_Biscuit_Time)

801.

Francisco Boix smuggled photographs out of the concentration camp Mauthausen and later on helped to convict SS-men in the Nuremberg trials.

Reference: (https://en.wikipedia.org/wiki/Francisco_Boix)

802.

The oldest working actor in Hollywood is Norman Lloyd at 103 years old.

Reference: (https://en.wikipedia.org/wiki/Norman_Lloyd)

803.

"Helicopter Money" is an unconventional monetary policy, similar to Quantitative Easing, where a Central Bank essentially gives money directly to the public.

Reference: (https://en.wikipedia.org/wiki/Helicopter_money)

804.

The Berlin Wall was opened accidentally. After being told the wrong information, a Soviet spokesman stated that border crossings would be allowed, "immediately". Crossings were actually planned to be allowed in limited circumstances. Thousands of East Germans then ran to the border and forced it open.

Reference: (https://www.reuters.com/article/us-germany-schabowski-obituary/guenther-schabowski-man-who-accidentally-opened-berlin-wall-dies-at-86-idUSKCN0SQ1T420151101)

805.

Detroit won a World Series, a Stanley Cup and the NFL Championship in 1935.

Reference: (https://en.wikipedia.org/wiki/Multiple_major_sports_championship_seasons)

806.

There is a linguistic zone in central France called "The Croissant."

Reference: (https://en.wikipedia.org/wiki/Croissant_(linguistic))

807.

There is a battery of unknown composition still supplying power after 176 years.

Reference: (https://en.wikipedia.org/wiki/Oxford_Electric_Bell)

808.

Flea and Dave Navarro played the guitar and bass on Alanis Morissette's "You Oughta Know".

Reference: (https://en.wikipedia.org/wiki/You_Oughta_Know)

809.

President Ulysses S. Grant was given a speeding ticket for driving his buggy "at a furious pace" through the streets of D.C.

Reference: (http://mentalfloss.com/article/65855/cop-who-gave-ulysses-s-grant-speeding-ticket)

810.

Chicago gets its drinking water from special intake stations in Lake Michigan, over 2 miles from the coast.

Reference: (https://en.wikipedia.org/wiki/Water_cribs_in_Chicago)

811.

Rapper Big Sean's grandmother was one of the first black female captains in World War II, and she also worked as a police officer in Detroit.

Reference: (https://www.billboard.com/articles/columns/the-juice/6415136/big-sean-grandma-dies)

812.

In Massachusetts, you can take home and eat any deer you hit yourself. In West Virginia, you can take any roadkill that isn't otherwise protected.

Reference: (https://news.nationalgeographic.com/2016/08/roadkill-animals-disposal-science-food/)

813.

The town of Whiteclay, Nebraska has a population of 14 people but beer sales at Whiteclay's four liquor stores totaled 4.9 million cans in 2010.

Reference: (https://en.wikipedia.org/wiki/Whiteclay%2C_Nebraska)

814.

In 2008, a 12-year-old boy in Florida was arrested for excessive farting in school.

Reference: (https://www.news.com.au/news/boy-arrested-for-farting-in-class/news-story/f8a925490b70543bb17e12ac2325a82e)

815.

The most unreliable model year of the Toyota Corolla was 2009.

Reference: (http://www.carproblemzoo.com/toyota/corolla/)

816.

There are still 9 living veterans of the Spanish Civil War, 7 Republicans and 2 Nationalists.

Reference:(https://www.wikipedia.org/wiki/List_of_surviving_veterans_of_the_Spanish_Civil_War)

817.

During World War II, the New Zealand minesweeper flotilla traded gin for 20 millimeter Oerlikon AA guns from the U.S. Navy.

Reference: (http://navymuseum.co.nz/history-of-the-rnzn-and-the-usn/)

818.

It is not clear what triggers lightning because the electrical fields in thunderclouds are not big enough to induce lightning discharge.

Reference: (http://www.bbc.com/future/story/20120926-what-causes-lightening)

819.

In 1999, Garry Kasparov played a chess match against 50,000 people over the Internet. He won and said it was his hardest game he played. Later, he revealed that he had been checking the opponents' discussion forum.

Reference: (https://en.wikipedia.org/wiki/Kasparov_versus_the_World)

820.

Norman Ernest Borlaug saved over a billion lives through improvements in farming.

Reference: (https://www.nobelprize.org/nobel_prizes/peace/laureates/1970/borlaug-bio.html)

821.

In 2015, Norma Bauerschmidt, a 90 years old woman was diagnosed with cancer. Instead of starting treatment, she, her son, daughter-in-law, and dog, went on a yearlong road trip around the U.S., travelling 13,000 miles around 32 states.

Reference: (https://www.npr.org/2016/10/07/497079353/driving-miss-norma-91-year-old-who-hit-the-road-after-cancer-diagnosis-dies)

822.

Chicken eyeglasses and contact lenses were in use as they acted as blinders, which help prevent fighting, pecking, and cannibalism among farmed chicken. This was an alternative to beak trimming practices.

Reference: (https://en.wikipedia.org/wiki/Chicken_eyeglasses)

823.

The Karaite Jews are an ancient sect hailing from Turkic countries. In 1934, members of the Karaite community asked the Nazis to exempt Karaites from the anti-Semitic laws based on their legal status as Russians, sparing them from the horrors of the Holocaust, despite them being fully Jewish.

Reference: (https://en.wikipedia.org/wiki/Crimean_Karaites#During_the_Holocaust)

824.

An American soldier, Henry Gunther, was the last casualty in World War I. He was killed at 10:59 AM, one minute before the Armistice was to take effect at 11 AM.

Reference: (https://en.wikipedia.org/wiki/Henry_Gunther)

825.

The U.S. Navy conducts regular Freedom of Navigation operations around the world to protect international trade and shipping from interference by any nation.

Reference: (https://en.wikipedia.org/wiki/Freedom_of_navigation)

826.

The small telescope on a tripod used by surveyors is called a theodolite, but nobody knows the history of that name.

Reference: (https://en.wikipedia.org/wiki/Theodolite#History)

827.

The United States exports the most sand in the world.

Reference: (https://www.worldatlas.com/articles/top-20-sand-exporting-countries.html)

828.

The most sued doctor in American history was Houston orthopedic surgeon Eric Scheffey, also known as Dr. Evil. He has been sued 78 times. At least five of his patients have died, and hundreds more have been seriously injured. It took 24 years for state regulators and the medical community to stop him.

Reference: (https://www.texasmonthly.com/articles/dr-evil///)

829.

Drachten, a town in the Netherlands, had almost all traffic lights and signs removed in the town's center in an effort to improve traffic safety, based on the theory that drivers pay more attention to their surroundings when they cannot rely on strict traffic rules.

Reference: (https://en.wikipedia.org/wiki/Drachten)

830.

Dogs that served with the U.S. Army in Afghanistan from 2010 to 2014 were poorly treated upon discharge, some were left in kennels for many months and not cared for, while others remain unaccounted. Several soldiers later searched for and rescued their ex-partners.

Reference: (https://www.reuters.com/article/us-usa-defense-dogs/canine-war-heroes-mistreated-by-u_s-army-pentagon-report-idUSKCN1GE30M)

831.

Many young Siberian girls are recruited to work as models in China because their European looks are in demand in the fashion industry.

Reference: (https://www.youtube.com/watch?v=GGK8I5m29tg)

832.

Randal Haworth, a Beverly Hills plastic surgeon who has appeared on TV shows like Fox's "The Swan," has been accused of illicit drug use and watching pornographic movies and videos depicting beheadings during his surgeries.

Reference: (https://www.thewrap.com/v-plastic-surgeon-randal-haworth-watches-porn-beheadings-drug-use-during-surgery-real-housewives/)

833.

The 1968 Summer Olympics were actually held in the middle of fall.

Reference: (https://www.olympic.org/mexico-1968)

834.

Alexander Kerensky, provisional President of Russia in 1917, later taught courses on the Russian Revolution at Stanford University where students would have to read their papers aloud to him and defend them.

Reference: (https://alumni.stanford.edu/get/page/magazine/article/?article_id=38883)

835.

Moscow Sheremetyevo Airport has a special express capsule hotel within its terminal where travelers can spend a night without a Russian visa.

Reference: (http://www.v-exp.ru/en/#)

836.

Madame C.J. Walker was the first black and the first female self-made millionaire in American history.

Reference: (https://www.biography.com/people/madam-cj-walker-9522174)

837.

Vincent Price made an impassioned plea against xenophobia and racism following a radio performance as The Saint in 1950.

Reference: (https://www.youtube.com/watch?v=I5afsN6KS_o&feature=youtu.be&t=26m10s)

838.

Atlantropa was a proposed mega-hydroelectric dam that would've, in theory, shrunken the Mediterranean, freeing up millions of square kilometers of new land to settle on while supplying power for most of mainland Europe.

Reference: (https://en.wikipedia.org/wiki/Atlantropa)

839.

The cross on top of the Holy Crown of Hungary was accidentally knocked crooked in the 17th century when the chest it was stored in was hastily closed. It was never repaired, and the crown has been displayed and depicted since then with its crooked cross.

Reference: (https://en.wikipedia.org/wiki/Holy_Crown_of_Hungary#Cross)

840.

In mass trauma situations, women of childbearing age are given priority for type O negative blood.

Reference: (https://www.bloodworksnw.org/medical-services/transfusion-medicine/emergency-red-blood-cell-use)

841.

In the U.S., there are 10 panhandle states and although Nebraska and Utah are similarly shaped, Nebraska is a panhandle state and Utah is not.

Reference: (https://www.nationalgeographic.com/travel/features/americas-panhandles-rated-oklahoma-florida/)

842.

Television was not introduced to South Africa until 1976.

Reference: (https://en.wikipedia.org/wiki/Television_in_South_Africa)

843.

In 1976, someone dubbed "The Circleville Letter Writer" began a campaign of harassment against the residents of Circleville, Ohio by mailing threatening letters containing personal information about the recipients.

Reference: (http://www.the13thfloor.tv/2017/01/04/the-mysterious-and-unexplained-incident-of-ohios_circleville-letters/)

844.

The last completed project of American painter Roy Lichtenstein was the logo of DreamWorks Records.

Reference: (https://en.wikipedia.org/wiki/Roy_Lichtenstein#Later_work)

845.

The Moon is 1/400th the size of the Sun but also 1/400th the distance from Earth, which results in the Moon and the Sun being the same size in the sky, a coincidence not shared by any other known planet-moon combination.

Reference: (http://earthsky.org/space/coincidence-that-sun-and-moon-seem-same-size)

846.

Between 1964 and 1973, the U.S. dropped two million tons of bombs on Laos.

Reference:(https://en.wikipedia.org/wiki/Laos?wprov=sfti1https://maps.apple.com/?ll=18.000000,105.000000&q=Laos&_ext=EiQpAAAAAAAMkAxAAAAAABAWkA5AAAAAAAMkBBAAAAAABAWkA%3D)

847.

In 1970, there were serious riots in Okinawa after a long series of crimes by American servicemen which went largely unpunished.

Reference: (http://www.japanupdate.com/2015/06/when-okinawa-was-no-so-peaceful-koza-riots-1970/)

848.

1 trillion species are estimated to be on Earth currently, with only one-thousandth of one percent described.

Reference: (https://en.wikipedia.org/wiki/Evolution)

849.

The "BB" in BB gun refers to the size of the projectile originally fired from them.

Reference: (https://en.wikipedia.org/wiki/BB_gun)

850.

There is no Korean last name "Lee"; rather, the second most common family name is "I", but since single letter names are so uncommon in English, almost all Koreans with that family name choose to go by Lee when representing their name in Roman characters.

Reference: (http://familypedia.wikia.com/wiki/Lee_(Korean_surname))

851.

Three of the nine known species of tigers went extinct during the 20th century; the Caspian Tiger, Javan Tiger, and the Bali Tiger.

Reference: (https://soapboxie.com/social-issues/How-to-Help-Protect-Endangered-Species)

852.

The 80 year old rumor of stores giving away free Tootsie Pops, when customers brought in a wrapper with a shooting star, was never endorsed by Tootsie Roll Industries.

Reference: (https://www.snopes.com/fact-check/shooting-star/)

853.

The last surviving soldier from World War I lived until the age of 111 years, 1 month, 1 week, and 1 day.

Reference: (https://en.wikipedia.org/wiki/Harry_Patch)

854.

The bristlecone pine forests in California has trees that are the oldest living organisms on the planet. At 4800 years old, some of the pines growing there today began growing before the pyramids were built.

Reference: (https://www.sierranevadageotourism.org/content/ancient-bristlecone-pine-forest/sieaa3468b39aae5045e)

855.

Northern pike fish feces contain alarm pheromones that scare other fish, such as the fathead minnow. While they could detect the pheromones to increase their chances of survival, northern pike will not defecate where they eat as a way to hide from being detected as the predator.

Reference: (https://youtu.be/Jiraiu-1uE0)

856.

The word "decimation" original referred to a form of Roman capital punishment against offending armies where every tenth solider in the legion was executed.

Reference: (https://en.wikipedia.org/wiki/Decimation_(Roman_army))

857.

Nikola Tesla was at the first party to have a stripper jump out of a cake.

Reference: (https://en.wikipedia.org/wiki/Pop_out_cake)

858.

Researchers from the Mayo Clinic argue that Michelangelo's painting the Creation of Adam depicts a postpartum uterus, not a brain.

Reference: (https://www.mayoclinicproceedings.org/article/S0025-6196%2815%2900153-6/fulltext?mobileUi=0)

859.

London still has around 1,500 gas street lights in operation.

Reference: (https://www.youtube.com/watch?v=HOZMAvzRjaM)

860.

Grandma Gatewood hiked the 2,200 mile Appalachian Trail at 55 bringing only Converse shoes, an army blanket and a plastic shower curtain after reading about it in a magazine and telling her children she was going for a walk. She hiked it again at 72 and 75.

Reference: (https://en.wikipedia.org/wiki/Grandma_Gatewood)

861.

Former president of Turkmenistan, Saparmurat Niyazov, decreed that January be named after him, and April after his mother.

Reference: (https://www.telegraph.co.uk/news/worldnews/asia/turkmenistan/1460852/A-peep-into-the-strange-world-of-Turkmenbashi-whose-every-word-is-law.html)

862.

Chiune Sugihara was a Japanese diplomat that saved 6,000 Jews during World War II by issuing them transit visas, risking his own career and life to save others.

Reference: (https://en.wikipedia.org/wiki/Chiune_Sugihara)

863.

Alaska has a rain forest.

Reference: (https://en.wikipedia.org/wiki/Tongass_National_Forest)

864.

Anthony Perkins died from AIDS on in 1992. His widow was killed on American Airlines Flight 11 on 9/11.

Reference: (https://abcnews.go.com/Entertainment/story?id=102505&page=1)

865.

In 1955, the Tokyo Tsushin Kogyo company leader Akio Morita explained that the company name would be difficult to pronounce in foreign lands. Changing it to Sony Corporation would allow them to expand worldwide.

Reference: (https://www.sony.net/SonyInfo/CorporateInfo/History/SonyHistory/2-23.html)

866.

In the 17th century, it was compulsory for boys at Eton School to smoke before breakfast for their health.

Reference: (https://www.telegraph.co.uk/comment/letters/3582724/Compulsory-smoking.html)

867.

The International Hair Freezing Contest is a sculpted hair competition held at a resort in the Takhini Hot Springs, Canada. The annual competition involves participants sitting in a hot spring and sculpting their wet hair in cold temperatures. The first place prize is $700 dollars.

Reference: (http://takhinihotpools.com/hair_freezing)

868.

In World War II, there was an army of 75,000 Chinese men stationed in Burma and trained by the American military to fight Japanese occupation in mainland Asia. They called these men, X Force.

Reference: (https://en.wikipedia.org/wiki/X_Force)

869.

Jack Ma, CEO of Alibaba Group starred in a short martial arts movie with many other well-known martial artists.

Reference: (https://www.youtube.com/watch?v=wfS9Uf5SKu8)

870.

The Greek question mark is a semicolon.

Reference: (http://questionmark.guide/greek-question-mark/)

871.

In China, Caucasian foreigners are hired to stand around and pretend to be an employee of the Chinese company or representative of an international company to increase the value of the Chinese company.

Reference: (https://www.vice.com/en_us/article/4wb84b/chinas-rent-a-foreigner-industry-is-still-a-real-thing)

872.

Sweden has a name for getting coffee called "Fika".

Reference: (https://en.wikipedia.org/wiki/Fika_(Sweden)#Definition)

873.

About 2% of fish routinely change from male to female.

Reference: (https://ourblueplanet.bbcearth.com/blog/?article=incredible-sex-changing-fish-from-blue-planet)

874.

There is a paper mill called Wookey Hole that has been in business for over 400 years in the U.K.

Reference: (https://en.wikipedia.org/wiki/Wookey_Hole_Caves)

875.

The most secure cryptological invention of World War II was SIGSALY, used by Churchill and Roosevelt to discuss war plans over a transatlantic radio link. The top secret equipment weighed 50 tons and drew 30 kW, about as much as 20 to 30 AC window units.

Reference: (https://en.wikipedia.org/wiki/SIGSALY)

876.

The red and white UN Honor Flag was occasionally flown during the final years of World War II to represent the solidarity of Allied Forces.

Reference: (https://en.wikipedia.org/wiki/United_Nations_Honour_Flag)

877.

It takes less than an hour to drive around the island of the Republic of Nauru. The most beautiful beaches there are not advised for swimming due to dangerous strong undercurrents.

Reference: (http://www.naurutourism.org/reservation)

878.

In the U.S., in 1944, there were 25.6 million dairy cows which produced 53 billion kilograms of milk. In 2007, there were only 9.8 million dairy cows, yet they produced 84.2 billion kilograms of milk.

Reference: (https://academic.oup.com/jas/article/87/6/2160/4731307)

879.

In 2009, the town of Docker River, Australia, was under siege by invasive nuisance camels. Out of thirst, 6000 camels smashed water mains, stampeded, and invaded the town's airstrip, until a massive camel slaughter reclaimed the town.

Reference:(https://www.telegraph.co.uk/news/worldnews/australiaandthepacific/australia/66596 74/Thirsty-camels-lay-siege-to-Australian-Outback-town.html)

880.

The eggs in "Alien" initially had a more vaginal appearance complete with an "inner and outer vulva". Producers worried that Catholic countries would ban the film, so Giger changed them so that, "seen from above, they would form the cross that people in Catholic countries are so fond of looking at."

Reference: (https://en.wikipedia.org/wiki/Alien_(creature_in_Alien_franchise)#Egg)

881.

When actor Ving Rhames won a Golden Globe in 1998, he called fellow nominee Jack Lemmon to the stage and gave him the award, saying, "I feel like being an artist is about giving, and I'd like to give this to you, Mr. Jack Lemmon."

Reference: (https://www.youtube.com/watch?v=Tk3EgDPZD0w)

882.

When they tried to book a phone call from the President to inform Sgt. Dakota Meyer that he had been approved for the Medal of Honor, White House staff were told he was working a construction job and to call back during his lunch hour.

Reference: (https://en.wikipedia.org/wiki/Dakota_Meyer)

883.

Acedia is a state of listlessness or torpor, of not caring or not being concerned with one's position or condition in the world; distinct from depression.

Reference: (https://en.wikipedia.org/wiki/Acedia)

884.

Seth Putnam, Founder of the band "Anal Cunt", chose said name for the band in an attempt, "to get the most offensive, stupid, dumb, etc. name possible."

Reference: (https://en.wikipedia.org/wiki/Anal_Cunt#Formation_(1988))

885.

Saint Peter, the first Pope, was crucified upside down at his own request, since he saw himself unworthy to be crucified in the same way as Jesus.

Reference: (https://en.wikipedia.org/wiki/Saint_Peter?2)

886.

During the World War II battle for the Coral Sea, the amount and magnitude of explosions was so intense that the reverberations caused the rubber bearings on some warship propeller shafts to harden and lock up, rendering the ships dead in the water.

Reference: (http://www.marineenginedigest.com/specialreports/cutless-bearings.htm)

887.

An orgasm can clear up your sinuses. This is because your body gets a rush of adrenaline when you have an orgasm, which causes tissues in the nose to shrink, opening up passageways.

Reference: (http://www.nbcnews.com/id/31213362/ns/health-sexual_health/t/ah-ah-ah-choo-orgasms-make-her-nose-stuffy/)

888.

The Battle of Attu is the only World War II battle fought in North America.

Reference: (https://en.wikipedia.org/wiki/Battle_of_Attu)

889.

The angle in which you cut a steak is integral to maintaining its proper texture.

Reference: (https://www.seriouseats.com/2010/03/why-should-you-cut-meat-steak-against-the-grain.html)

890.

Vulfpeck released a completely silent ten song album on Spotify called "Sleepify". The ten songs each last roughly thirty seconds. The band asked fans to play the album as they slept to generate royalties and go on tour.

Reference: (https://en.wikipedia.org/wiki/Sleepify)

891.

The majority Muslim country of Albania saved countless Jewish lives during World War II. Under the oath of "Besa", a uniquely Albanian code of honor, a guest in one's home must be protected at all costs, even if it means laying down your life for your guest.

Reference: (http://religion.blogs.cnn.com/2012/08/03/documentary-seeks-to-explain-why-albanians-saved-jews-in-holocaust/)

892.

The "Tamworth Two" was a pair of pigs that escaped from a truck headed for a slaughterhouse in England. They were on the run for a week before they were eventually caught. The Daily Mail newspaper bought the pigs, which were then sent to an animal sanctuary to live out their lives.

Reference: (https://en.wikipedia.org/wiki/Tamworth_Two)

893.

The Richard Mille RM69 is an erotic luxury watch with a 69 hour power reserve. The exact pricing is tough to find, but apparently it cost approximately 690,000 CHF.

Reference: (https://www.ablogtowatch.com/richard-mille-rm-69-erotic-tourbillon-watch/)

894.

Not only do traffic lights have sensors to detect when you arrive at an intersection, but also that "dead red" laws allow cyclists to run red lights if the sensors fail to pick them up.

Reference:(https://en.wikipedia.org/wiki/Traffic_light#%22Dead_Red%22_laws_for_motorcycles)

895.

In 1985, a private party sold 1.5 million shares of Apple causing a 12-year low. This helped Steve Jobs in a proposal that Apple oust CEO Gil Amelio and he became the replacement. It was later revealed that the privately sold 1.5 million shares, which is worth over $60 billion today, was sold by Steve Jobs.

Reference: (http://www.businessinsider.com/steve-jobs-original-apple-stock-would-be-worth-66-billion-today-2016-4)

896.

Angelina Jolie once hired a hitman to kill her because she felt being murdered would be easier on her family than her suicide. The hitman gave her time to reflect, though, and she changed her mind.

Reference: (https://www.shared.com/angelina-jolie-hitman/)

897.

A "Moon rock" given to Holland by Neil Armstrong and Buzz Aldrin is fake.

Reference: (https://www.telegraph.co.uk/news/science/space/6105902/Moon-rock-given-to-Holland-by-Neil-Armstrong-and-Buzz-Aldrin-is-fake.html)

898.

Holocaust survivor Eva Mozes Kor had her parents ripped from her and killed in a Nazi death camp when she was only a child, and was subject to human experimentation with her twin sister. She later came to forgive the same Nazis that tortured her.

Reference: (https://en.wikipedia.org/wiki/Eva_Mozes_Kor)

899.

Judges need not have a law degree or law experience to become a judge.

Reference: (https://www.howtobecome.com/how-to-become-a-judge)

900.

The Kamikaze Attacks deployed by Japan during World War II were much better than conventional air attacks, with a success rate of about 19%.

Reference: (https://www.japantimes.co.jp/news/2015/03/03/national/two-kamikaze-pilots-two-late-reprieves-one-pacifist-view/)

901.

Maggots can help with healing wounds in part because they suppress the body's immune system, helping keep inflammation down.

Reference: (http://www.sciencemag.org/news/2012/12/how-maggots-heal-wounds)

902.

"Fart Proudly", also called "A Letter to a Royal Academy About Farting", and "To the Royal Academy of Farting", is the popular name of an essay about flatulence written by Benjamin Franklin circa 1781 while he was living abroad as the United States Ambassador to France.

Reference: (http://wikipedia.org/wiki/Fart_Proudly)

903.

Junk mail produces 1 billion pounds of landfill each year.

Reference: (https://blog.hubspot.com/blog/tabid/6307/bid/3741/5-shocking-statistics-how-junk-mail-marketing-damages-the-environment.aspx)

904.

Stan Lee had a contract awarding him 10% of the net profits of anything based on his characters. The first Spider-Man made more than $800 million in revenue, but the producers claimed it did not make any profit and Lee received nothing.

Reference: (https://en.wikipedia.org/wiki/Hollywood_accounting)

905.

24 rabbits released in Australia in October of 1859 have multiplied to be in excess of 200 million, causing havoc to native flora and fauna.

Reference: (https://en.wikipedia.org/wiki/Rabbit_plagues_in_Australia)

906.

When Sultan Mohammed V of Morocco was commanded to round up all Moroccan Jews for relocation to Nazi concentration camps, he said, "There are no Jews in Morocco. There are only Moroccan subjects." Not a single Moroccan Jew was deported or killed during World War II.

Reference: (http://www.latimes.com/opinion/op-ed/la-oe-hurowitz-moroccan-king-mohammed-v-20170425-story.html)

907.

Wirth's Law states that, "Software manages to outgrow hardware in size and sluggishness". It was formulated in 1995 by the Turing award-winner Niklaus Wirth and it observed exponential growth in hardware cost and performance in 1965.

Reference: (https://en.wikipedia.org/wiki/Wirth%27s_law)

908.

The blue Jelly Bean was created for Ronald Reagan.

Reference: (http://jellybelly.com/cgi-bin/MsmGo.exe?grab_id=11&page_id=11927552&query=ronald+reagan&MSCSProfile=2B46F2608C8456A38DA1611543879EB9FEE0C4EA3754AFFFD6204CDC7898F515B8AE302C55E

0E3A3FD5AFC9E7837AE2BA332EDFA1484AEE454F64B63D988FB1A742D8EBEBA6F64 C2063BAA743830)

909.

Mellow Yellow is a song about an electrical, vibrating, banana designed for female sexual pleasure.

Reference: (https://en.wikipedia.org/wiki/Mellow_Yellow)

910.

"2001: A Space Odysseys'" director Stanley Kubrick wanted to take out insurance with Lloyd's to protect himself against losses in the event that extraterrestrial intelligence was discovered before his movie was released. Lloyd's refused.

Reference: (https://www.lloyds.com/about-lloyds/history/innovation-and-unusual-risks/wild-and-woolly)

911.

When you look at a second hand on a clock, the first tick will appear to last longer because your brain is attempting to stitch together reality.

Reference: (https://www.mnn.com/green-tech/research-innovations/stories/mystery-solved-why-clocks-seem-to-stop-ticking-the-second)

912.

The Pulfrich Effect is the effect that makes a video 3D and 2D at the same time. This happens because of each frame in a video, but you have to have the camera moving for it to take effect.

Reference: (https://www.youtube.com/watch?v=Q-v4LsbFc5c)

913.

Ronald Reagan received an electoral vote in 1976, four years before receiving the Republican nomination.

Reference: (https://en.wikipedia.org/wiki/United_States_presidential_election,_1976)

914.

Egypt's last king was 6 months old when he ascended to the throne.

Reference: (https://en.wikipedia.org/wiki/Fuad_II_of_Egypt)

915.

There's a musical road in Lancaster, California that is supposed to play William Tell Overture but it is out of tune.

Reference: (https://www.youtube.com/watch?v=Ef93WmlEho0)

916.

Wang Yan, a former millionaire steel factory proprietor, forfeited his fortune and went bankrupt to rescue dogs. He says the loss of his dog compelled him to open a dog rescue service, and he has helped rescue over 2,000 stray dogs.

Reference: (https://en.wikipedia.org/wiki/Wang_Yan_(activist))

917.

The English subtitles for "Pan's Labyrinth" were translated and written by Guillermo del Toro himself. He no longer trusts translators after having encountered problems with his previous subtitled movies.

Reference: (https://en.wikipedia.org/wiki/Pan%27s_Labyrinth?repost#Subtitles)

918.

Jeff Goldblum, the actor, was nominated for an Academy Award, but it was for a film he directed.

Reference: (https://en.wikipedia.org/wiki/Jeff_Goldblum)

919.

"Dark Side of the Moon" was recorded with quadraphonic in mind.

Reference: (http://www.goldminemag.com/articles/pink-floyds-dark-side-of-the-moon-quadraphonic-eight-track-sells-for-676)

920.

When interacting with someone of "higher status" than oneself, they generally use the pronoun "I" significantly more than the other person during the dialogue.

Reference: (https://hbr.org/2011/12/your-use-of-pronouns-reveals-your-personality)

921.

There's a pictorial script older than Egyptian hieroglyphs from the Indus Valley Civilization, but it's currently undecipherable.

Reference: (https://en.wikipedia.org/wiki/Indus_script)

922.

There are versions of "The Office" in Sweden, Finland, Czech Republic, France, Quebec, Germany, Chile, Israel, and India. They all sell paper except for Germany, which sold insurance.

Reference: (https://www.bbc.com/news/entertainment-arts-43113390)

923.

Researchers investigated the belief that cocaine use causes weight loss by appetite suppression and found that it's false. They discovered that cocaine users actually eat more than non-users, but also that they store significantly less fat mass despite eating more.

Reference: (https://www.elementsbehavioralhealth.com/featured/the-skinny-on-cocaine-why-drug-causes-weight-loss-may-surprise-you/)

924.

The Finnish Air Force used the Swastika as their symbol from 1917 to 1945.

Reference: (https://en.wikipedia.org/wiki/Finnish_Air_Force#History)

925.

Lord Darrell Duppa named and co-founded what is now Phoenix, Arizona. His house still stands to this day.

Reference: (https://en.wikipedia.org/wiki/Phillip_Darrell_Duppa)

926.

Even though cocaine use has either dropped or stayed the same in most of the U.S., it's still a major problem in Hollywood, where snorting a line at a party can be as commonplace as drinking a glass of wine.

Reference: (http://www.foxnews.com/entertainment/2011/07/29/addicted-in-hollywood-stars-problems-with-cocaine-still-going-strong.html)

927.

Malarial mosquitoes helped defeat the British Army in the battle that ended the Revolutionary War. Not having access to many doctors, some soldiers resorted to folk remedies like eating spiders, drinking their own urine, or tying their hair to tree trunks and yanking it to get the disease out.

Reference: (https://www.smithsonianmag.com/science-nature/how-lowly-mosquito-helped-america-win-independence-180959411/)

928.

Germany's Christoph Kramer got such a bad concussion during a game that he forgot he was playing in the FIFA World Cup Final 2014.

Reference: (https://www.theguardian.com/football/2014/jul/17/christoph-kramer-germany-concussion-world-cup-final-2014)

929.

During the first infamous defenestration of Prague, seven members of the city council were defenestrated and killed. Upon hearing this news, King Wenceslaus IV of Bohemia was stunned and died, supposedly due to the shock of the incident.

Reference: (https://en.wikipedia.org/wiki/Defenestrations_of_Prague#cite_note-Catholic_Encyclopedia-1)

930.

In 1925, the Ku Klux Klan contributed $25 each to the Volunteers of America and African Methodist Episcopal Church, which was supposed to prove the KKK wasn't anti-black.

Reference:(https://en.wikipedia.org/wiki/Ku_Klux_Klan_recruitment#Charity_work_and_recruitment)

931.

Raindrops are not tear-shaped but actually shaped like the top of a hamburger bun.

Reference: (https://pmm.nasa.gov/education/videos/anatomy-raindrop)

932.

The Hidden Holocaust, better known as the "Congo Horrors", was caused by King Leopold II of Belgium. The magnitude of the population fall over the period is disputed, but it is thought to be as high as 15 million people.

Reference: (https://en.wikipedia.org/wiki/Atrocities_in_the_Congo_Free_State)

933.

In 1762, Prussia was losing hard in the 7 Years' War and Russians were close to capturing Berlin, however, after the death of the Russian Empress Elizabeth, her successor, Peter III, just changed his mind and signed a peace with Prussia thus allowing them to concentrate their effort against Austria.

Reference: (https://en.wikipedia.org/wiki/Seven_Years%27_War#1761%E2%80%9362)

934.

It took until 1820 for humans to discover the continent of Antarctica. It was also the last region on Earth in recorded history to be discovered.

Reference: (http://www.south-pole.com/p0000052.htm)

935.

Sponsianus was a supposed challenger to the Roman throne. His only evidence is a single coin with his image that is widely thought to be a fake.

Reference: (https://en.wikipedia.org/wiki/Sponsianus)

936.

The iconic Batman television series with Adam West only ran 3 season, but had 120 episodes with season 2 having 60.

Reference: (https://en.wikipedia.org/wiki/Batman_(TV_series))

937.

During the beginning of the Cold War, the USSR penetrated the Los Alamos nuclear lab in the U.S. and stole sensitive information. At the end of the Cold War, China penetrated the same lab and stole information of the most advanced miniaturized U.S. nuke and replicated it and improved it.

Reference: (https://www.nytimes.com/1999/03/06/world/breach-los-alamos-special-report-china-stole-nuclear-secrets-for-bombs-us-aides.html)

938.

Sounds typical of disordered speech, such as those caused by lisps or head colds, are represented by their own set of symbols as "extensions to the International Phonetic Alphabet".

Reference: (https://en.wikipedia.org/wiki/Extensions_to_the_International_Phonetic_Alphabet)

939.

The iconic theme from "The Twilight Zone" was actually 2 separate pieces of stock music written for use in CBS shows by an avant-garde composer, who didn't know it was being used as a theme song and didn't get any royalties from it.

Reference: (https://en.wikipedia.org/wiki/Marius_Constant)

940.

"Eggcorns" are commonly misheard phrases that retain their original meaning.

Reference: (http://grammarist.com/mondegreens/)

941.

The Bohemian Rhapsody video took only four hours to film. The band arrived to the studio at 7:30 in the morning and by 11:30 they were finished and were relaxing in a local pub. The entire thing cost $2,025.

Reference: (http://mentalfloss.com/article/70634/10-operatic-facts-about-bohemian-rhapsody)

942.

The English beat the Spanish fleet by initiating their final battle via 8 burning ships called fireships to disrupt their tight fleet. The Greeks did something similar; Known as the Napalm of the ancient times, this technology was called Greek Fire.

Reference: (https://www.ancient.eu/)

943.

All six members of Monty Python tried for the role of Wonka in "Willy Wonka and the Chocolate Factory." Three were even seriously considered for the role in the 2005 film.

Reference: (https://en.wikipedia.org/wiki/Willy_Wonka_%26_the_Chocolate_Factory#Casting)

944.

Walton Goggins knocked out his front teeth twice as a kid.

Reference: (https://www.youtube.com/watch?v=0CxApTXyTxU&feature=youtu.be)

945.

An earworm is a catchy piece of music that continually repeats through a person's mind after it is no longer playing and can be cured by chewing gum.

Reference: (https://en.wikipedia.org/wiki/Earworm)

946.

Sandra Laing was a South African woman who was classified as colored by authorities during the apartheid era, due to her skin color and hair texture, although she was the child of at least three generations of ancestors who had been regarded as white.

Reference: (https://en.wikipedia.org/wiki/Sandra_Laing)

947.

Early engineers secretly defied Steve Jobs by hiding their, successful, collaboration with Sony on the 3.5" floppy drive.

Reference:(https://www.folklore.org/StoryView.py?project=Macintosh&story=Hide_Under_Thi s_Desk.txt)

948.

Marriages can have postnuptial agreements.

Reference: (https://en.wikipedia.org/wiki/Postnuptial_agreement)

949.

In 2005, Flight 522 crashed into the mountains near Athens, Greece, killing all 122 passengers and 6 crew members. It was known as the "Ghost Flight". All crew, except 1, and passengers were unconscious for the last 164 minutes of the flight.

Reference: (https://en.wikipedia.org/wiki/Helios_Airways_Flight_522)

950.

The proud owner of the first silicone breast implant was a dog called Esmeralda.

Reference: (https://www.bbc.co.uk/news/magazine-17511491)

951.

F.F.E. Yeo-Thomas, a British SOE agent, escaped Soviet Russian capture by strangling a guard, dined with infamous Nazis to gather intel, and was subjected to brutal torture by the Gestapo during World War II. Ian Fleming would use Yeo-Thomas as inspiration for his fictional character, James Bond.

Reference: (https://en.wikipedia.org/wiki/F._F._E._Yeo-Thomas)

952.

Ottoman sultan Murad III was impotent. According to historians, "his arrow was working but was unable to reach the target of union and pleasure." After many attempts by his mother, a cure was found with one side effect: his libido increased so much by the end of his reign he had over 100 children.

Reference: (https://en.wikipedia.org/wiki/Murad_III#Palace_life)

953.

John Wayne smoked 6 packs of cigarettes a day.

Reference: (https://en.wikipedia.org/wiki/The_Conqueror_(1956_film)#Cancer_controversy)

954.

Running a mile only burns 105 net calories.

Reference: (https://www.runnersworld.com/nutrition-weight-loss/a20825897/how-many-calories-are-you-really-burning-0/)

955.

NASA has named "Gattaca" as the most accurate science fiction film of all time.

Reference: (https://www.theatlantic.com/entertainment/archive/2011/01/nasa-calls-2012-silliest-sci-fi-film-of-all-time-says-jurassic-park-is-scientifically-plausible/69049/)

956.

Stendhal syndrome is a psychosomatic disorder that causes rapid heartbeat, dizziness, fainting, confusion and even hallucinations when an individual is exposed to an experience of great personal significance, particularly viewing art.

Reference: (https://en.wikipedia.org/wiki/Stendhal_syndrome)

957.

The CPU from the original PlayStation guided a probe to Pluto.

Reference: (https://www.theverge.com/2015/1/15/7551365/playstation-cpu-powers-new-horizons-pluto-probe)

958.

"Zuo Tang" was a Chinese wedding ritual sometimes practiced in the Sichuan Province. Every day for one hour, one month prior to the wedding, the bride goes into a hallway and cries, with her mother, grandmother, sisters and aunts eventually joining in.

Reference: (http://www.odditycentral.com/pics/strange-wedding-customs-the-crying-ritual-of-the-tujia-people.html)

959.

Although he was only 42 years old when assassinated, Robert Kennedy had 10 children during his life, and one more born after his death.

Reference: (https://www.vanityfair.com/magazine/1997/08/kennedykids199708)

960.

Gregor Mendel, the founder of modern genetics, may have falsified data in his famous pea experiment in order to better correspond with his expectations.

Reference: (https://www.thegreatcoursesdaily.com/gregor-mendel-fake-data/)

961.

The Bdelloid Rotifers are the most radiation-resistant animals, capable of withstanding hundred times the radiation that would kill a human.

Reference: (http://phenomena.nationalgeographic.com/2008/03/24/bdelloid-rotifers-the-worlds-most-radiation-resistant-animals/)

962.

Former Ugandan president Idi Amin called himself: "His Excellency, President for Life... Lord of All the Beasts of the Earth and Fishes of the Seas and Conqueror of the British Empire in Africa in General and Uganda in Particular", in addition to his claim of being uncrowned King of Scotland.

Reference: (https://en.wikipedia.org/wiki/Idi_Amin#Erratic_behaviour,_self-bestowed_titles_and_media_portrayal)

963.

The first mechanical shower, which was operated by hand pump, was patented by stove maker William Feetham, in England in 1767.

Reference: (https://en.wikipedia.org/wiki/Shower#Modern_showers)

964.

The average cumulus cloud weighs 1.1 million pounds, about the same as 100 elephants.

Reference: (http://mentalfloss.com/article/49786/how-much-does-cloud-weigh)

965.

Joseph Stalin was an accomplished poet and several of his poems became minor Georgian classics.

Reference:(https://www.theguardian.com/books/2007/may/19/featuresreviews.guardianreview32?CMP=Share_iOSApp_Other)

966.

Evidence suggests that "brainstorming" is counter-productive, and produces fewer original ideas than when individuals work alone.

Reference: (https://hbr.org/2015/03/why-group-brainstorming-is-a-waste-of-time)

967.

When the Chinese leaders ordered generals to use military force to quash the protests, one refused, saying it was a political problem that should be settled by negotiation. He was arrested and over 1000 students were shot.

Reference: (https://www.nytimes.com/2014/06/03/world/asia/tiananmen-square-25-years-later-details-emerge-of-armys-chaos.html)

968.

The satisfying clunk when you close a car door is a fake sound.

Reference: (https://oodlecarfinance.com/five-fake-car-sounds-to-make-the-vehicle-sound-better/)

969.

Octopuses have eight arms, rather than tentacles.

Reference: (https://en.wikipedia.org/wiki/Cephalopod_limb)

970.

The Benz Patent Motor Car was the first automobile ever.

Reference: (https://www.daimler.com/company/tradition/company-history/1885-1886.html)

971.

The estimated probability for human extinction before 2100 is 19%.

Reference: (https://en.wikipedia.org/wiki/Global_catastrophic_risk#Likelihood)

972.

A boy legally changed his name when he was eight years old to Loki Skylizard; today he is a surgeon and goes by Dr. Skylizard.

Reference: (http://drskylizard.com/skylizard/)

973.

One way biological immortality can be attained is by preventing downregulation of the complex Telomerase in somatic cells. In humans, it's only found in large numbers in stem and cancer cells, but in other organisms, it's found in all tissues and some of them have the potential to live forever.

Reference: (https://www.ncbi.nlm.nih.gov/pubmed/11193292)

974.

People on the island of Yap, near Japan, use giant limestone disks, some weighing several tons as currency.

Reference: (https://www.npr.org/sections/money/2011/02/15/131934618/the-island-of-stone-money)

975.

Chinese "Ghost Cities," are cities meant to hold millions of people but are practically empty.

Reference: (https://www.wired.com/2016/02/kai-caemmerer-unborn-cities/)

976.

The name of the mall in "Back to the Future" changed from Twin Pines Mall to Lone Pine Mall in later scenes because Marty hit a tree on Old Man Peabody's farm shortly after arriving in 1955.

Reference: (https://geektyrant.com/news/2010/5/25/did-you-ever-notice-this-twin-pines-mall-easter-egg-in-back.html)

977.

London's "Continuum Magazine" promoted the idea that HIV was a social construct created to stigmatize gays, until it shut down after all its editors died of AIDS.

Reference: (https://newhumanist.org.uk/2165/how-to-spot-an-aids-denialist)

978.

Pronoia, the opposite of paranoia, is the delusion that everyone is secretly plotting your success.

Reference: (http://www.pronoia.net/def.html)

979.

Stan Freberg, who replaced Jack Benny on CBS radio in 1957, refused to allow tobacco manufacturers as sponsors, despite it being an impediment to his career.

Reference: (https://en.wikipedia.org/wiki/Stan_Freberg)

980.

Scientists discovered human-sized penguin fossils in New Zealand; the birds were over 200 pounds and almost 6 feet tall.

Reference: (https://relay.nationalgeographic.com/proxy/distribution/public/amp/2017/12/human-size-penguin-fossil-discovered-new-zealand-spd)

981.

Female tennis player Esther Vergeer went on a decade long winning streak in wheelchair singles ended only by her retirement. Her streak lasted 470 matches and brought her 7 Paralympic gold medals and 21 grand slam singles titles.

Reference: (https://www.nytimes.com/2013/02/13/sports/wheelchair-tennis-champion-esther-vergeer-retires.html)

982.

During the filming of the famous egg eating contest in the movie "Cool Hand Luke", Paul Newman never actually swallowed any eggs. Instead they put a trash can next to Newman and he would spit out the eggs every chance he got.

Reference: (http://www.icepop.com/cool-hand-luke/)

983.

Seinfeld ended the last episode with the same bit as the beginning of the pilot episode.

Reference: (https://www.youtube.com/watch?v=RN2BagUS0ko&feature=youtu.be)

984.

Madagascar wildlife is so unique that over 90% of it are endemic species that can't be found anywhere else on Earth. The reason for that is the fact that it has been isolated for 88 million years from other land masses.

Reference: (https://en.wikipedia.org/wiki/Wildlife_of_Madagascar)

985.

Peter Freuchen was an Arctic explorer who, after getting trapped by an avalanche, used his feces to fashion a dagger to free himself.

Reference: (https://en.wikipedia.org/wiki/Peter_Freuchen#Career)

986.

As a result of being raised in a very religious household, Axl Rose was not only a choir boy in his youth, but also a Sunday School teacher.

Reference: (http://www.iheartradio.ca/news/25-things-you-may-not-know-about-birthday-boy-axl-rose-1.2384651)

987.

There is an estimated 2 to 30 million insect species in the world and of that only 900,000 are known. Insects have the largest biomass of terrestrial animals and at any time it is estimated that there are 10 quintillion individual insects alive.

Reference: (https://www.si.edu/spotlight/buginfo/bugnos)

988.

J.J. Burnel, singer and bassist from punk band The Stranglers, is the head of the U.K. branch of Shidokan karate.

Reference: (http://thequietus.com/articles/14627-stranglers-jj-burnel-interview)

989.

"The East Is Red" was the national anthem of China during the Cultural Revolution in the 1960s. The lyrics of "The East Is Red" idealize Mao Zedong, and Mao's popularization of "The East Is Red" was one of his earliest efforts to promote his image as a perfect hero in Chinese popular culture.

Reference: (https://en.wikipedia.org/wiki/The_East_Is_Red_(song))

990.

Over half of new car sales now in Norway are electric or hybrid.

Reference: (https://www.reuters.com/article/us-environment-norway-autos/norway-powers-ahead-over-half-new-car-sales-now-electric-or-hybrid-idUSKBN1ES0WC)

991.

B95 or Moonbird was a 21 year old Red Knot who has flown the same distance from the Earth to the Moon and back in his lifetime. He is also the oldest known example of the species earning him the title of the "Toughest 4 Oz on the Planet."

Reference: (https://www.mnn.com/earth-matters/animals/stories/this-20-year-old-bird-has-flown-to-the-moon-and-back)

992.

The smallest "country" to compete in the 2018 FIFA World Cup qualifiers is Montserrat. It only has a population of 5,000 people, a 3rd of the island is cut of due to a volcano, it only has one airport and most of their players are born in England.

Reference: (http://www.fifa.com/worldcup/preliminaries/nccamerica/index.html)

993.

90% of the Aral Sea, the 4th largest lake in the world, evaporated and is now a desert, mainly due to the Soviet ambition of turning Central Asia into the largest cotton producer in the world.

Reference: (http://www.bbc.co.uk/news/resources/idt-a0c4856e-1019-4937-96fd-8714d70a48f7)

994.

For years, the launch code to U.S. nuclear missiles was "00000000" so that it was quicker to fire them.

Reference: (https://www.youtube.com/watch?v=vnGlbb_9CYY)

995.

Because almost all cheetahs were wiped out by the last Ice Age, modern cheetahs are all practically genetic clones of each other.

Reference: (https://www.smithsonianmag.com/science-nature/rare-breed-20811232/)

996.

Because medicine is seen as women's work in Russia, their doctors aren't paid well.

Reference: (https://themoscowtimes.com/news/russian-doctors-paid-less-than-fast-food-workers-57667)

997.

The Ottoman Sultan wrote to a group of Ukrainian Cossacks in 1676 and demanded their submission. They responded, "We have no fear of your army, by land and by sea we will battle with thee, fuck thy mother."

Reference: (https://en.wikipedia.org/wiki/Reply_of_the_Zaporozhian_Cossacks)

998.

Microsoft had a social network, it was called So.cl, and it operated between 2011 and 2015.

Reference: (https://techcrunch.com/2017/03/07/microsoft-socl-close/)

999.

Numbness, and sometimes temporary paralysis, caused from falling asleep on your arm is a result of nerve compression and not loss of blood flow to the limb.

Reference: (https://www.vox.com/2016/6/6/11854588/numb-arm-sleep)

1000.

In Norway, about 17,000 men have Leif as their first, or only, name. In Sweden, 70,000 men have the name Leif, about 60% of them as a first name.

Reference: (https://en.wikipedia.org/wiki/Leif)

Printed in Great Britain
by Amazon

71848950R00092